PRESENTED TO

MARES MEMORIAL LIBRARY

BY

MARES MEMORIAL LIBRARY

IN HONOR OF

DELEON SAND & GRAVEL

4/01

Science Projects About
Solids, Liquids, and Gases

Titles in the **Science Projects** *series*

Science Projects About
Solids, Liquids, and Gases

Robert Gardner

Mares Memorial Library
4324 Highway 3
Dickinson, TX 77539

Enslow Publishers, Inc.

40 Industrial Road	PO Box 38
Box 398	Aldershot
Berkeley Heights, NJ 07922	Hants GU12 6BP
USA	UK

http://www.enslow.com

Library of Congress Cataloging-in-Publication Data

Gardner, Robert, 1929–
    Science projects about solids, liquids, and gases / Robert Gardner.
        p. cm. — (Science projects)
    Includes bibliographical references and index.
    Summary: Presents science projects and experiments exploring the states of matter,
their properties, and their measurement.
    ISBN 0-7660-1168-2
    1. Matter—Properties—Experiments Juvenile literature. 2. Science projects Juvenile
literature. [1. Matter—Experiments. 2. Experiments. 3. Science projects.] I. Title.
II. Series: Gardner, Robert, 1929– Science projects.
QC173.16.G37 2000
507'.8—dc21   99-42737
                                        CIP

Printed in the United States of America

10 9 8 7 6 5 4 3 2

To Our Readers:
All Internet addresses in this book were active and appropriate when we went to press. Any
comments or suggestions can be sent by e-mail to Comments@enslow.com or to the address
on the back cover.

Illustration Credits: Enslow Publishers, Inc., pp. 18, 19, 20, 21, 22, 26, 37, 49,
61, 65, 72, 76, 79, 86, 102, 114, 117, 119; Stephen F. Delisle, pp. 14, 23, 38, 41,
48, 53, 56, 71, 82, 84, 89, 91, 94, 108, 109, 111, 120.

Cover Illustration: Jerry McCrea (foreground); © Corel Corporation (background).

Contents

*appropriate ideas for science fair project

*appropriate ideas for science fair project

Introduction

All matter exists in one of three states—solid, liquid, or gas.* This book is filled with projects and experiments related to these states. You will find that you can learn many interesting facts about matter by doing the experiments. Most of the materials you will need to carry out your investigations can be found in your home, a hardware store, or a supermarket. For a few experiments, you may want to borrow equipment or chemicals from your school's science department. If the school's policy prevents your teachers from letting you take equipment home, you can probably carry out these experiments at school during free time.

For some of the experiments, you will need one or more people to help you. It would be best if you work with friends or adults who like to do experiments as much as you do. In that way, you will all enjoy what you are doing. If any danger is involved in doing an experiment, it will be clearly stated in the text. **In some cases, to avoid any danger to you, you will be asked to work with an**

Plasma is a fourth state of matter found in and between stars, but we will not consider it in this book.

adult. Please do so. We do not want you to take any chances that could lead to an injury.

Like a good scientist, you will find it useful to record your ideas, notes, data, and anything you can conclude from your experiments in a notebook. By so doing, you can keep track of the information you gather and the conclusions you reach. Record keeping will allow you to refer to experiments you have done, which may help you in doing other projects in the future. In some of the experiments, you will have to make some calculations. Therefore, you may find it helpful to have a calculator nearby as you do these experiments and analyze the data you collect.

Science Fairs

Most of the projects in this book are appropriate for a science fair. These projects are indicated with an asterisk (*). However, judges at such fairs do not reward projects or experiments that are simply copied from a book. For example, plugging numbers into a formula you do not understand will not impress judges. A graph of data collected from experiments you have done that is used to find a relationship between two variables would be more likely to receive serious consideration.

Science fair judges tend to reward creative thought and imagination. It is difficult to be creative or imaginative unless you are really interested in your project. So be sure to choose a subject that appeals to you. And before you jump into a project, consider, too, your own talents and the cost of materials you will need.

If you decide to use a project found in this book for a science fair, you should find ways to modify or extend it. This should not be difficult, because you will probably discover that as you do these projects new ideas for experiments will come to mind—experiments that could make excellent science fair projects, particularly because the ideas are your own and are interesting to you.

8

If you decide to enter a science fair and have never done so before, you should read some of the books listed in the bibliography, as well as *Science Fair Projects—Planning, Presenting, Succeeding*, which is one of the books in this series. These books deal specifically with science fairs and will provide plenty of helpful hints and lots of useful information that will enable you to avoid the pitfalls that sometimes plague first-time entrants. You will learn how to prepare appealing reports that include charts and graphs, how to set up and display your work, how to present your project, and how to relate to judges and visitors.

Safety First

Most of the projects included in this book are perfectly safe. However, the following safety rules are well worth reading before you start any project.

1. Do any experiments or projects, whether from this book or of your own design, under the supervision of a science teacher or other knowledgeable adult.

2. Read all instructions carefully before proceeding with a project. If you have questions, check with your supervisor before going any further.

3. Maintain a serious attitude while conducting experiments. Fooling around can be dangerous to you and to others.

4. Wear approved safety goggles when you are working with a flame, using a hammer, or doing anything that might cause injury to your eyes.

5. Do not eat or drink while experimenting.

6. Do not go on a frozen lake or pond without permission from an adult.

7. Have a first-aid kit nearby while you are experimenting.

8. Do not put your fingers or any object other than properly designed electrical connectors into electrical outlets.

9. Never experiment with household electricity except under the supervision of a knowledgeable adult.

10. Do not touch a lit high wattage bulb. Lightbulbs produce light, but they also produce heat.

11. Many substances are poisonous. Do not taste them unless instructed to do so.

12. If a thermometer breaks, inform your adult supervisor. Do not touch either the mercury or the broken glass with your bare hands.

1

Matter: Gases, Liquids, and Solids

Matter is anything that has mass and takes up space. This book is matter, your body is matter, the water you drink is matter, the air you breathe is matter.

Mass is a measure of the amount of matter. Mass can usually be found with a balance or scale. There is a difference between mass and weight. Mass is the amount of matter in an object. It is the same everywhere. If your mass is 50 kilograms (kg), it will be 50 kg on the moon or anywhere else. Your weight is the force with which gravity pulls on you. Newtons are the units used to measure force. If your mass is 50 kg, you will weigh nearly 500 newtons (N) (110 pounds) on the earth. Any mass of 50 kg will weigh nearly 500 N on the earth. On the moon, where gravity is weaker, you would weigh only about 80 N (18 pounds), but your mass would still be 50 kg. There is no less of you on the moon than on the earth, but the moon does not pull as hard on you as the earth does.

Since all the experiments in this book are to be done on the earth, the difference between mass and weight will not usually be important. Consequently, mass units will be used throughout. Occasionally, when gravity plays a role, we will use the term *weight* instead of mass. We will express the force of gravity in units of grams-weight (g-wt) or kilograms-weight (kg-wt) so you will not have to deal with newtons. Newtons are probably less familiar to you than grams or kilograms.

The amount of space a chunk of matter occupies is known as its volume. Volume can be found in a number of different ways, as you shall see.

1-1
The States of Matter

Matter comes in three states—solid, liquid, or gas. Most of the things we handle in our daily lives are solids, but nearly three fourths of the earth we live on is covered by a liquid—water! Above the earth's land and seas is an invisible blanket of gas more than 100 kilometers thick. This gas is the air that makes up earth's atmosphere. Air is actually a mixture of gases, mostly nitrogen (78 percent) and oxygen (21 percent).

Things you will need:
- wood block
- glass of water
- glass, cup, or pan with a different shape than the first glass
- balloon
- twist-tie
- plastic syringe
- water
- dry sand

A block of wood can serve as a typical solid. Does it have a definite shape? Does it have a fixed (unchanging) volume? As long as no force acts on the solid, does either its shape or volume change?

Water is a liquid. Pour some water into a glass, cup, or pan. Then pour it into a container with a different shape. Does a liquid have a definite shape? Or does it take the shape of the container it is in? As long as none of the water is allowed to evaporate, is its volume fixed?

Air can serve as a typical gas. Blow some air into a balloon and seal its neck with a twist-tie. Can you change the shape of the gas in the balloon? Does a gas have a fixed shape? Or does it take the shape of the container it is in? Now remove the twist-tie so the air can escape. Does a gas have a fixed volume? Where is the gas that left the balloon?

Another way to examine some properties of a gas is with an empty plastic syringe. As shown in Figure 1a, lift up the plunger to draw some air into the syringe. Place your finger over the end of the syringe and push the plunger farther into the cylinder as shown in Figure 1b. Did you change the shape of the gas? Did you change

13

its volume? What happens if you keep your finger tightly against the open end of the syringe and release the plunger?

Were you able to compress a gas—that is, squeeze it into a smaller volume? Try the same thing with water. Draw about half a cylinderful of water into the syringe. Place your finger tightly against the open end of the cylinder and try to push the plunger inward. Can you compress a liquid?

Do you think you can compress a solid? To find out, fill the cylinder of a plastic syringe with dry sand. Place your finger over the open end, then try to push the plunger down. Can you compress a solid?

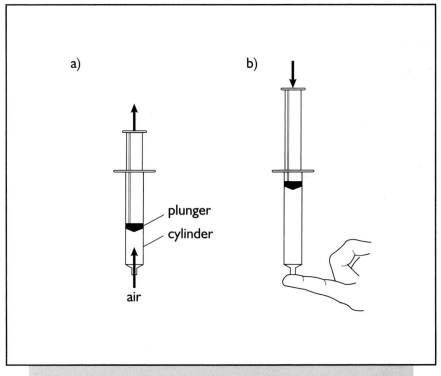

Figure 1. a) Pull the plunger of a syringe outward to draw air into the cylinder. b) Put your finger firmly over the open end of the syringe and push the plunger inward. Can you squeeze air into a much smaller volume?

An Atomic Model of Matter

To explain the different states of matter and other chemical properties, an English chemist named John Dalton developed an atomic model of matter early in the nineteenth century. According to his atomic theory, elements are the basic substances. They consist of identical particles called atoms. Hydrogen, oxygen, iron, aluminum, carbon, and so on, are elements. The atoms of any one element are identical, but the atoms of different elements differ in mass. The mass of oxygen atoms, for example, is 16 times as massive as hydrogen atoms, $\frac{4}{3}$ as massive as carbon atoms, but only $\frac{1}{2}$ as massive as sulfur atoms.

Compounds are substances formed by the chemical joining of two or more elements. The atoms of different elements sometimes combine, always in a fixed ratio, to form molecules. Molecules are the fundamental particles that make up compounds. For example, two atoms of hydrogen combine with one atom of oxygen to form a molecule of water.

In a gas, the atoms or molecules are far apart, in constant motion, and free to move virtually independently of one another. Because the particles of a gas are so far apart, a certain volume of gas has far less mass than the same volume of a liquid or solid. The large distance between gas molecules makes it possible to compress a gas—squeeze it into a much smaller volume. And because gas molecules are in constant motion, they will fill any enclosed space in which they are placed.

In a liquid, the molecules or atoms are touching but are free to move around one another. Because the molecules of a liquid are close together, a liquid cannot be compressed. However, the molecules can slide around one another and, therefore, can take the shape of any vessel into which they are poured.

Solids are of a fixed shape and volume because, as with liquids, their atoms or molecules are touching one another. Unlike liquids, the molecules of a solid are not free to move about one another.

They are in fixed positions and can only vibrate in place. Since the fundamental particles of a solid are in fixed positions, the shape of a solid remains the same regardless of where it is placed.

There is experimental evidence to show that the speed at which atoms and molecules move is related to their temperature. When heat is added to matter, the average speed of the molecules that make up that matter increases. Even the atoms or molecules in solids vibrate more rapidly as their temperature rises. In fact, the kinetic energy of molecules—the energy associated with their motion—can be shown to be in proportion to temperature.

1-2*
Measuring the Volume of Matter

Things you will need:

Using scissors, a ruler, and a pencil, cut a square 1.0 centimeter (cm) on a side from a piece of light cardboard. The upper surface of the square has an area that is defined as 1.0 square centimeter (cm^2). The area of a square or rectangle is length times width, and 1.0 cm x 1.0 cm = 1.0 cm^2. Now pull the square over a distance of 1.0 cm, as shown in Figure 2, to sweep out a volume. The volume swept out by the square is 1.0 cm^3 (cubic centimeter). The volume of a regular solid is equal to the area of its base times its height, and 1.0 cm^2 x 1.0 cm = 1.0 cm^3.

Things you will need:

- scissors
- ruler
- pencil
- light cardboard
- modeling clay
- graduated cylinder
- olive jar
- marking pen
- masking tape
- stone that will fit in the graduated cylinder
- water
- dishpan
- sink
- a partner
- balloon

The volume you swept out was a cube, because its length, width, and height were all equal. Use some clay to make a solid cube that is 1.0 cm in length, width, and height. What is the volume of the cube? Show that the total surface area of all the sides of the cube is 6.0 cm^2.

As shown in Figure 3, the volume of any regular solid is given by the formula:

Volume = area of base (length x width) x height, or $V = lwh$.

In order to find the volume of matter in a cylinder, you will need to use a formula that includes π (pi), which is the ratio of a circle's circumference to its diameter. Its value is approximately 3.14. The volume of a cylinder (see Figure 4) is $\pi r^2 h$, where r is the radius of

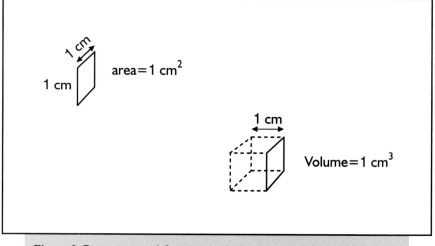

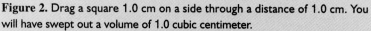

Figure 2. Drag a square 1.0 cm on a side through a distance of 1.0 cm. You will have swept out a volume of 1.0 cubic centimeter.

the base of the cylinder, h is its height, and π is approximately 3.14. The number you attach to a volume depends on the units used to measure the radius and the height. You could use inches just as well as centimeters, or yards as well as meters. In this book, we will use metric units (millimeters, centimeters, meters, etc.) throughout because the metric system is used for most scientific measurements.

The volume of regular solids, such as cubes, cylinders, and rectangular solids (parallelepipeds) can be found by multiplying the area of the base by the height. But how can you find the volume of a solid with an irregular shape such as a stone?

To understand how the volume of a stone can be measured, you need to first see how the volume of a liquid can be measured. As you saw in Experiment 1-1, a liquid has no fixed shape. It takes the shape of the vessel into which it is poured. We can use this property of liquids to determine their volumes. Usually, this is done by pouring the liquid into a hollow cylinder called a graduated cylinder. A graduated cylinder, like the one in Figure 5, has horizontal lines along its side that are used to measure the volume of its contents.

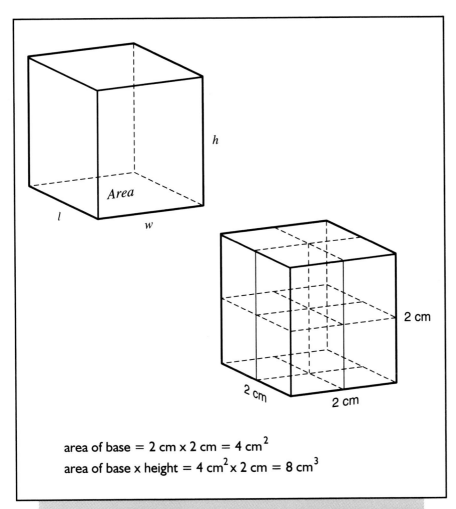

area of base $= 2\ \text{cm} \times 2\ \text{cm} = 4\ \text{cm}^2$
area of base x height $= 4\ \text{cm}^2 \times 2\ \text{cm} = 8\ \text{cm}^3$

Figure 3. The volume (V) of any regular solid is equal to the area of the base (*l* x *w*) times the height (*h*); consequently, V = *lwh*. As an example: 2 cm x 2 cm x 2 cm = 8 cm³. Notice that each layer contains 4 cubic centimeters. There are two layers for a total of 8 cm³.

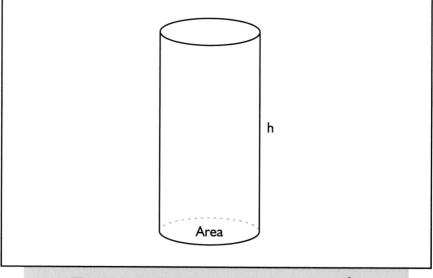

Figure 4. Show that the volume of a cylinder is equal to $\pi r^2 h$.

Suppose the cylinder has a diameter of 3.57 cm. Its radius (1.785 cm), when squared and multiplied by π, is 10.0 cm². If the horizontal lines on the side of such a graduated cylinder are spaced 1.0 cm apart, the space between lines is 10 cm³, because 10.0 cm² x 1.0 cm = 10 cm³.

You may find that a commercially made graduated cylinder is marked in milliliters (mL). A milliliter, as its name indicates, is $\frac{1}{1,000}$ of a liter (L). It has the same volume as a cubic centimeter (1 cm³ = 1 mL). Therefore, 1,000 mL and 1,000 cm³ both equal 1.0 L.

Make a graduated cylinder using a tall glass cylinder, such as a jar that olives come in. To prevent the lines from being rubbed off, attach a vertical strip of masking tape to the side of the jar and make the marks on the tape. Mark a zero (0) line at the bottom of the tape. Carefully measure the diameter and calculate the cross-sectional area of the jar. Then use a marking pen and ruler to make lines that correspond to 10 mL intervals above the 0 line.

Figure 5. The cylinder shown here is graduated into intervals of 1.0 cm³ or 1.0 mL.

When you have finished making your graduated cylinder, you can check it in a school lab. Pour known volumes of water from a graduated cylinder or metric measuring cup into the graduated cylinder you made. Be sure you use the bottom of the curved meniscus (see Figure 6) to measure the volume. Water adheres to glass or plastic so that a thin ring of water in contact with the glass rises higher than the rest of the water. The actual volume of the water is below the bottom of the meniscus.

How closely does the volume measured in the commercial graduated cylinder agree with the volume as measured in your homemade one?

You can now find the volume of a solid with an irregular shape, such as a stone. Two different pieces of matter cannot occupy the same space. With a graduated cylinder, you can measure the volume of an irregular solid. Note the exact volume of some water in a graduated cylinder. Then carefully lower the stone into the cylinder.

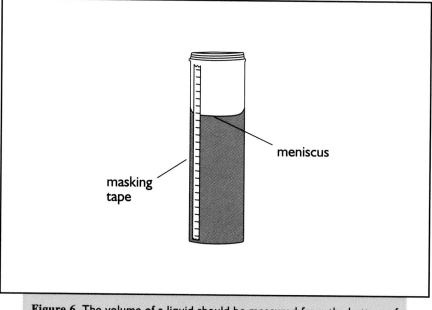

Figure 6. The volume of a liquid should be measured from the bottom of the meniscus.

What happens to the water level? How much water did the stone displace? What is the volume of the stone?

The volume of many gases can be measured in the same way. To do this, get a partner to join you. You will need a balloon. Add several inches of water to a dishpan in a sink. Then fill a graduated cylinder with water, cover the top of the cylinder with a cardboard square, hold the square firmly against the cylinder as you invert it and place it in the pan of water, as shown in Figure 7a. Have your partner hold the cylinder in place while you put the neck of an inflated balloon under the mouth of the graduated cylinder in the dishpan. Partially release the neck of an inflated balloon so that bubbles of air rise up the graduated cylinder (see Figure 7b). As you can see, the gas replaces the water in the cylinder. How much air was in the balloon? How could you measure the volume of a large volume of gas, a volume larger than the volume of the graduated cylinder?

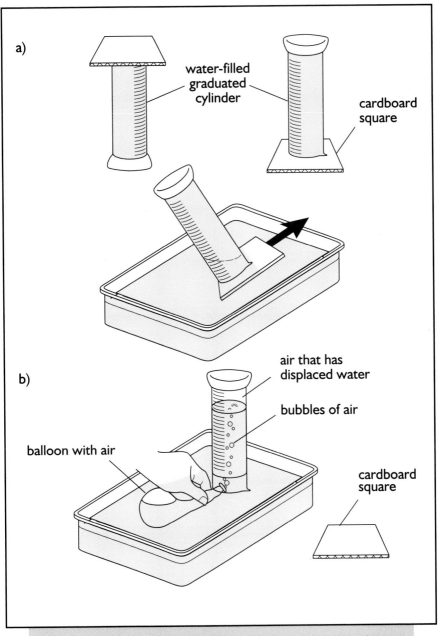

a)

water-filled
graduated
cylinder

cardboard
square

b)

air that has
displaced water

bubbles of air

balloon with air

cardboard
square

Figure 7. a) Cover the mouth of a graduated cylinder with a cardboard square. Then invert the cylinder and place its covered mouth under water. b) Allow gas from a balloon to displace water from the graduated cylinder.

Exploring on Your Own

Design an experiment to measure the volume of air that you normally inhale and exhale during breathing. Then find the largest amount of air that you can exhale after taking a deep breath.

How would you measure the volume of a gas that dissolves in water?

Show that the surface area of a cylinder is $2\pi r^2 + 2\pi rh$.

Show that the volume of a cone is $\frac{1}{3}\pi r^2 h$, where r is the radius of the cone's circular base and h is the vertical height of the cone.

Demonstrate that the volume of a sphere is $\frac{4}{3}\pi r^3$, where r is the radius of the sphere.

1-3*
Measuring the Mass in Matter

If you have a balance or scale, you can use it to measure mass. If not, you can make one from a yardstick, aluminum pie tins, string, a nail, and paper clips.

Ask an adult to drill three small holes through a wooden yardstick, as shown in Figure 8a. The hole at the 18-inch mark should be slightly above the center of the yardstick. A hole one inch from each end of the balance should be 0.25 inch above the lower side of the yardstick. Slide a finishing nail snugly through the middle hole to serve as a pivot point for the balance beam (yardstick). Opposite ends of the pivot nail can rest on two large sand-filled cans set on a bench or small table.

Things you will need:

• wooden yardstick

• string

• an adult

• drill and bits

• ruler

• finishing nail

• 2 large cans

• sand

• bench or small table

• 2 large paper clips

• string

• aluminum pie tins

• clay

• small paper clips or washers

• two 30-mL plastic medicine cups

• eyedropper

Next, open two large paper clips. Slip the wider end of each paper clip through the holes at the ends of the balance beam. String can be used, as shown, to hang small pie tins from the paper clips at each end of the beam (Figure 8b). If the balance beam is not level after the pans are in place, add a small piece of clay to the lighter (turned-up) side. Move the clay along the top of the balance beam until it is level.

You can now use the balance to weigh a variety of small objects by seeing how much mass you must place in the right-hand pan to balance the object in the left-hand pan.

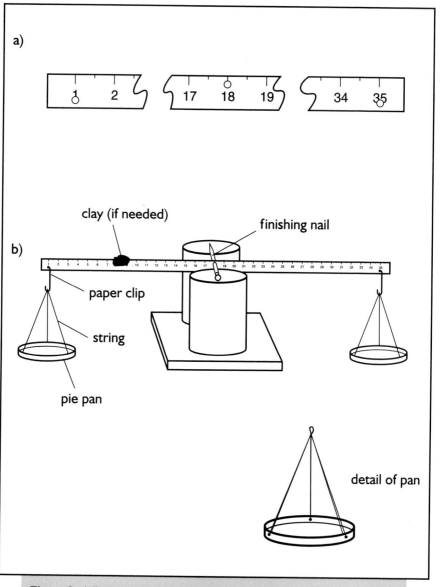

Figure 8. a) Drill three holes through a wooden yardstick, as shown. A nail through the center hole can serve as a pivot for the balance beam. b) Add pans, and you have made a sensitive balance.

Since you probably do not have a standard set of gram masses, you can use identical paper clips or small washers as your unit of mass. To convert these masses to grams, you will have to find out how many paper clips or washers equal one gram. You can do this by placing identical empty 30-mL plastic medicine cups on opposite pans of the balance. If the beam is not level, move the clay until it is level. Use an eyedropper and another calibrated medicine cup or graduated cylinder to add exactly 20 mL of water to the medicine cup on the left-hand pan.

The mass of 20 mL of water is 20 grams (g). To determine the mass of a single paper clip or washer, add these small masses to the right-hand pan of your balance until they balance the 20 g of water on the other pan. It will probably require about 40 paper clips to balance 20 g of water. The number of washers will depend on their size.

If the last paper clip or washer you add tips the balance beyond its level position, place that paper clip on the beam, as you did the clay, and move it until balance is achieved. How can you use that paper clip to make an accurate measurement of the mass of the water to the nearest fraction of a paper clip unit? Whatever your measurement in paper clips, it is equal to 20 g. How can you use the information you have just obtained to find the mass of one paper clip in grams?

Use your balance to measure a number of different solids and liquids. What is the smallest mass your balance can measure? Can you measure the mass of a drop of water? If not, can you measure the mass of ten drops? Of 100 drops? How can you use the mass of 100 drops to find the mass of one drop?

Exploring on Your Own

In building your balance, you were told to make the center hole at the 18-inch mark *above* the center of the balance beam. The pans were hung 0.25 inch above the *bottom* of the beam. To explore the effect of the position of the center and end holes on a balance, you can use a piece of pegboard about 17 inches long by 2 inches wide with small holes about ½ inch apart. The pegboard balance beam should be a little more than three holes wide and 35 holes long. It can be suspended from a nail driven into a post or upright board. Large paper clips can be used to suspend the pans from the ends of the beam. Vary the positions of the center pivot and the suspension positions of the pans. How and why do the positions of the pivot point and pan suspensions affect the balance?

See if you can build a balance that will measure very small masses such as a postage stamp. Then see if you can build a balance that will measure large masses such as you and your friends.

One of the fundamental laws of nature is the law of conservation of mass, which states that mass cannot be created or destroyed. **Under adult supervision,** design and carry out experiments to show that mass is conserved during chemical reactions as well as during physical changes such as melting and freezing.

1-4
Mass and Inertia

Inertia is the quality of a body that maintains its state of motion. Anything that has mass has inertia. Isaac Newton clari-

Things you will need:

• hard-boiled egg

• uncooked egg

fied how objects move in his laws of motion. According to the first law of motion, an object at rest will remain at rest unless a force acts on it. If the object is in motion, it will continue to move at a steady speed in the same direction unless a force acts on it.

But suppose you are riding your bike along a level path and you stop pedaling. You do continue to move; however, your speed gradually decreases until you come to rest. Does this mean the first law of motion is wrong?

No, nothing is wrong with the law. You slow down and finally come to rest because there is a force acting against your motion. That force is the friction between the bicycle tires and the road and between you and the air.

While the laws of motion apply to all states of matter—solid, liquid, or gas—there are differences. Remember, the molecules of a liquid are free to move around one another, but the molecules of a solid are in fixed positions and not free to move. To see how this difference can affect motion, you will need two eggs, one hard-boiled and one uncooked.

Place the hard-boiled egg on a counter and set it spinning about a fixed point. Suddenly stop the egg's rotation with your hand and then immediately release it. As you might expect, the egg remains at rest after you free it.

Next, set the uncooked egg spinning in the same way. Then stop it just as you did the hard-boiled egg. Does the egg remain at rest, or does it continue to rotate slowly after you release it? How can you explain the difference in the behavior of these two spinning eggs after they are stopped?

1-5*

Mass and Volume Together: The Density of Liquids and Solids

The ability to measure volume and mass provides you with a way to determine a characteristic property that can be used to help identify substances. That property is density—a measure of the compactness of matter. It tells you how much matter is packed into a certain volume. Density is defined as mass divided by volume.

To find the density of a substance, you need to weigh a known volume of that substance. For example, you might find that a piece of cork with a volume of 100 cm³ weighs 25 g. You would calculate its density to be 0.25 g/cm³ because:

$$\frac{25 \text{ g}}{100 \text{ cm}^3} = 0.25 \text{ g/cm}^3.$$

Things you will need:

- balance you made in Experiment 1-3 or suitable substitute
- metric ruler
- block of wood, lump of clay, and other solids such as steel washers and pieces of metal such as copper, brass, aluminum, coins, etc.
- different kinds of wood (pine, balsa, maple, oak, etc.)
- pen or pencil
- notebook
- graduated cylinder or metric measuring cup
- liquids: water, rubbing alcohol, vinegar, fruit juices, milk, Gatorade, molasses, baby oil, and cooking oil
- an adult if you use liquids other than those listed

To obtain the information needed to determine the density of a solid with a regular shape, you can simply measure its dimensions with a ruler, calculate its volume, and then weigh it. How would you find the density of a solid with an irregular shape, such as a lump of clay?

To find the density of a liquid, you can weigh an empty graduated cylinder or metric measuring cup. Then add a known volume of liquid to the cylinder or cup and weigh again. How can you use these measurements to find the density of the liquid?

One liquid whose density is very useful for scientific purposes is water. Water is used as a standard for many other measurements such as mass, heat, temperature, solubility, acidity, and density.

Design an experiment to determine the density of water. Take into consideration the accuracy of your balance and graduated cylinder or measuring cup when deciding what volume to use. For example, if you can measure volume to only the nearest milliliter, you certainly want to use more than 10 mL of water. An error of 1 mL in 10 mL means you can only measure to ± 10 percent (1 part in 10 parts). Generally, you want to weigh as large a volume as is practical so that you can be as accurate as possible. For example, an error of 1 mL in 100 mL enables you to measure volume to within one percent. The same is true of mass; the larger the mass, the less the error. Of course, you have to take into account the limitations of the available instruments. A large graduated cylinder may not fit on your balance, and a balance is limited by the mass it can accommodate.

Generally, 100 cm^3 of a liquid or solid will provide sufficient accuracy. With a balance that can measure to one-tenth of a gram, 10 mL will be sufficient if the volume can be measured to one-tenth of a cubic centimeter.

Taking the accuracy of your measuring tools into account, determine the density of a block of wood, a lump of clay, and a variety of other solids. Steel washers, pieces of copper, brass, aluminum, and other metals such as coins may be available. You can also use different kinds of wood (pine, balsa, maple, oak, etc.). As you work, record your measurements and calculations in a notebook.

Which solid was the densest? Which was the least dense? Of the woods you measured, which was the most dense? Which was the least dense?

Now turn your attention to liquids. Remember to measure their volume using the bottom of the meniscus. After confirming that the density of water is 1.0 g/cm^3, you might measure the masses of known volumes of a number of other liquids that may be available. Rubbing alcohol, vinegar, fruit juices, milk, Gatorade, molasses, baby oil, and cooking oil are good choices. **Check with an adult** before trying other liquids. Again, record your measurements and calculations in a notebook.

Exploring on Your Own

The density of isopropyl alcohol (isopropanol) is 0.79 g/cm^3. Isopropanol is the main ingredient in rubbing alcohol. What did you find the density of rubbing alcohol to be?

Examine the label on the bottle of rubbing alcohol you used. What fraction of the liquid is isopropanol? Assuming the other ingredient is water, what would you expect the density of rubbing alcohol to be? How does that value compare with the density you calculated from your measurements? How might you explain any differences between the density expected and the density calculated?

Before a standard metal kilogram weight was established, a liter of water served as a suitable substitute. Show that the mass of one liter of water is 1.0 kg.

Investigate how water is used as a standard for other measurements such as heat, temperature, solubility, acidity, and density.

Does the amount of matter affect a substance's density? That is, would the density of 100 mL of water be different from the density of 200 mL?

1-6
Density and Floating

Do you think the density of a solid can be used to determine whether it will sink or float in water?

To find out, use what you learned in the previous experiment in which you measured the densities of a number of differ-

Things you will need:

• lump of clay that weighs about 50 grams

• balance you built in Experiment 1-3 or another balance or scale

• water

• metric measuring cup

ent solids. Take those solids that are more dense than water and place them in water. Do they sink or float? Then take those solids that are less dense than water and place them in water. Do they sink or float? What can you conclude?

What about steel ships? You probably found that steel is more dense than water. Nevertheless, steel ships float in water. Perhaps you can understand why they float by doing another experiment.

Prepare a lump of clay that weighs about 50 grams. You can weigh the clay on the balance you built in Experiment 1-3 or on another balance or scale. Next, add about 200 mL of water to a metric measuring cup. Place the lump of clay in the measuring cup. How much water does the clay displace? What is the volume of the clay?

According to the measurements you have made, what is the density of the clay? Does the density of clay that you just determined agree with the density you calculated for clay in the previous experiment?

Now reshape the lump of clay. Mold it into a dish-shaped vessel with high sides. Note the water level in the metric measuring cup. Then carefully lower the clay onto the water in that cup. If the clay does not float, remove it and mold it some more until it will float. Once the clay floats, note the water level in the cup. How much water does the clay displace now? How many grams would that volume of water weigh? How does the weight of the water displaced compare with the weight of the clay?

Using what you have learned, see if you can explain why steel boats can float. (You will learn more about floating in the next chapter.)

2

Finding the Mass and Density of Gases

We think of gases as being light substances and solids as being heavy. However, a roomful of air might weigh 40 kilograms or more. A solid coin, such as a nickel, weighs only 5 grams. If we weigh *equal* volumes of a solid and a gas, their differences are more apparent. A cubic centimeter of nickels weighs 8.9 grams. The same volume of air weighs only 0.0012 grams.

In Chapter 1, you measured the volumes and masses of solids and liquids. You also found a way to measure the volume of a gas that does not dissolve in water. Measuring the mass of a gas is more complicated because, as you will see, its mass is affected by the air in which it is weighed.

2-1
Measuring the Mass of Air

Try to find the mass of some air by weighing it. If you are using the balance described in Experiment 1-3, follow the directions below. If you are using a different kind of balance, such as an electronic or triple-beam balance, you need to weigh a plastic bag

Things you will need:
- balance from Experiment 1-3 or appropriate substitute
- plastic bags (1 gallon or larger) and very large plastic bags such as trash bags
- twist-ties

(1 gallon or larger) and twist-tie when the bag is empty and again when it is filled with air and sealed with the twist-tie.

To use the balance you built in Experiment 1-3, remove the pans and use twist-ties to hang two identical plastic bags (1 gallon or larger) from opposite ends of the balance. Both bags should be collapsed; that is, neither bag should hold any air. If the balance beam is not level, move the small lump of clay along the beam until it is. Now remove the bag from one end of the beam and drag it through the air to fill it with gas. Then hang the air-filled bag back on the balance. Does the air appear to have any mass?

Perhaps there was too little air to affect the balance. Try using much larger plastic bags, such as trash bags. Does a larger volume of air appear to have any mass?

Does air really have no mass? How can it be that the air you feel pushing against you when the wind blows, when you ride your bicycle, or when you hold your hand out a moving car window has no mass? Perhaps the answer can be found by doing a similar experiment with water.

2-2
Measuring the Mass of Water in Air and in Water

You know that water has mass; you have probably weighed it many times. But did you ever weigh water *in water*? After all, you tried to weigh air in air. To find the mass of water in water, you can use either the balance you built in Experiment 1-3 or a spring balance.

Things you will need:

- balance you built in Experiment 1-3 or a spring balance
- plastic sandwich bags
- water
- twist-ties
- a partner, if you use the balance you built in Experiment 1-3
- pail

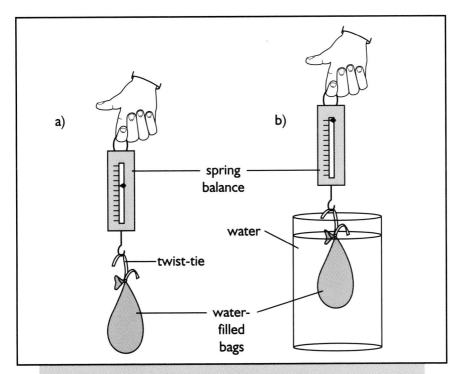

Figure 9. a) A water-filled bag is weighed in air. b) The same bag is weighed while submerged in water.

37

If you use a spring balance, partially fill a plastic sandwich bag with water. Twist the top of the bag to close off the water. Be sure there are no air bubbles trapped with the water, then seal it shut with a twist-tie. Use the end of the twist-tie to hang the bag of water from a spring balance, as shown in Figure 9a. What is the mass of the bag and the water?

Now lower the bag of water hanging from the spring balance into a pail of water (Figure 9b). What is the mass of the water when weighed in water?

If you use the balance you built in Experiment 1-3, you will need a partner to help you. Obtain two identical plastic sandwich bags and twist-ties. Be sure they have the same mass by hanging them from the paper clips at opposite ends of your balance. If they are not quite the same, move the lump of clay until the beam is level. Next, fill one plastic bag with water. Twist the top of the bag to close off the water. Be sure there are no air bubbles trapped inside, then seal it shut with a twist-tie. Have your partner hold the balance

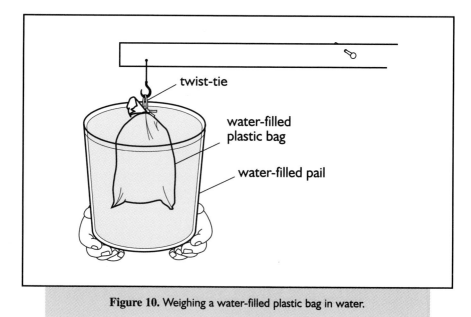

twist-tie

water-filled
plastic bag

water-filled pail

Figure 10. Weighing a water-filled plastic bag in water.

beam while you hang the bag of water from one end of the balance. Have your partner continue to keep the balance beam level while you raise a pail of water under the bag of water until it is submerged, as shown in Figure 10. Then have your partner release the beam. What is the mass of water when weighed in water? How does it compare with the mass of air when weighed in air?

2-3*
Measuring the Mass of a Solid in Water

Things you will need:

• clay

• balance you made in Experiment 1-3 or a spring scale

• string

• glass of water

• paper clips or gram masses

As you saw in the previous experiment, the mass of water when weighed in water is zero. The same is true of air weighed in air. Would a solid weigh less if weighed in water?

To find out, you can weigh a large ball of clay in air and then in water. Again, you can do this by using a spring scale or the balance you made in Experiment 1-3.

Wrap a large piece of clay around a length of string. If you are using a spring scale, tie a loop in the string and hang the clay from the spring scale. What is the mass of the clay in air? Now weigh the clay while suspended in a glass of water. What is the clay's apparent mass in water?

If you are using the balance you made in Experiment 1-3, have a partner hold the balance beam while you attach the clay to one end of the balance beam. What is the mass of the clay in paper clips and grams? Now repeat the experiment with the clay suspended in a glass of water that you hold beneath one end of the balance beam, as shown in Figure 11. How much does the clay weigh in water?

Since more than ⅔ of your body is water, how do you think your weight in water would compare with your weight in air?

Exploring on Your Own

Design an experiment to determine your weight while submerged in water. Then carry out your experiment **under adult supervision**.

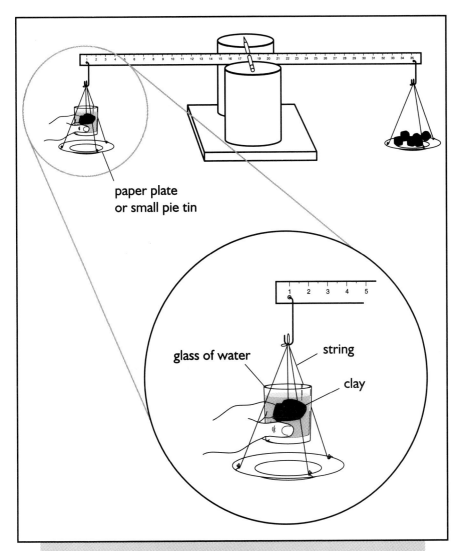

paper plate
or small pie tin

glass of water

string

clay

Figure 11. Does the apparent mass of a lump of clay change if it is weighed in water?

Archimedes and Buoyancy

The Greek philosopher Archimedes (287–212 B.C.) was one of the few Greek philosophers who actually did experiments. One of his experiments occurred quite unexpectedly.

Archimedes had been trying to figure out a way to measure the volume of an irregularly shaped object. The irregular shape was the king's crown. The king thought he might have been cheated. He had asked Archimedes to find out whether the crown was made of pure gold. To find the density of the crown, and thus determine if it was solid gold, Archimedes needed to know its volume.

While getting into his bath, Archimedes suddenly realized that a solid object displaces its own volume when submerged in a liquid. According to legend, he leaped from the bath and ran naked through the streets, shouting, "*Eureka! Eureka!*" In Greek, *eureka* means "I have found it!"

Archimedes' realization that the volume of a solid could be found by immersing it in a liquid led him to another discovery. His careful experiments revealed that a solid object in a liquid is buoyed up (lifted) by a force equal to the weight of the liquid it displaces. Later experiments showed that gases, too, provide buoyancy.

His discovery about buoyancy is known today as Archimedes' Principle: *A body in a fluid (liquid or gas) is buoyed up (lifted) by a force equal to the weight of the fluid it displaces.*

You can repeat the experiment that led Archimedes to understand buoyancy. In so doing, you will learn why air appears to have no mass when weighed in air and why the same is true of water weighed in water.

2-4*
Checking Up on Archimedes' Buoyancy Idea

Use a sensitive spring balance (0–250 grams or 0–2.5 newtons) or the balance you made in Experiment 1-3 to weigh a solid, such as a piece of metal or clay. The solid should have a reasonably large volume (20–50 cm^3). Find the volume of the solid by immersing it in some water in a graduated cylinder or a metric measuring cup. How much water does it displace? What is the volume of the solid object?

Next, weigh a volume of water equal to the volume displaced by the solid. Finally, weigh the solid while submerged in water, as shown in Figure 9 and Figure 11.

Things you will need:

• spring balance (0–250 grams or 0–2.5 newtons) or the balance you made in Experiment 1-3

• solid such as a metal or clay with volume of 20–50 cm^3

• water

• graduated cylinder or metric measuring cup

• small container

• string

• several different solids with different volumes

• rubbing alcohol

How does the solid's weight when submerged in water compare with its weight in air? How does its loss of weight in water compare with the weight of the water it displaces?

Repeat the experiment several times, using different solids with different volumes. Are your results similar in each case? As accurately as your measurements allow, try to decide whether the solid's loss of weight in water equals the weight of the water displaced.

Do you think Archimedes' Principle works with other liquids? To find out, try the same experiment using rubbing alcohol in place of water. What do you find?

Why did water appear to have no mass when you weighed it in water? What evidence do you have to show that Archimedes' Principle applies to gases as well as to liquids?

Exploring on Your Own

A liter (1,000 cm^3) of air has a mass of 1.2 grams. What is the apparent loss of mass when a 27-gram piece of aluminum, which has a volume of 10 cm^3, is weighed in air? How could you detect such a weight loss?

Place an egg in a pint-sized jar that is nearly filled with water. The egg sinks. Add a heaping tablespoonful of salt to the water and stir. Why does the egg now float? Can you find a way to make the egg float in the *middle* of the jar?

2-5
Measuring the Mass of Gases

As you have seen, air appears to have no mass when weighed in air. And water appears to have no mass when weighed in water. Archimedes' Principle explains why air weighed in air and water weighed in water both appear to be weightless. Each is buoyed up by the weight of the fluid they displace. Since a volume of air displaces its own volume, it is buoyed up by its own weight and so appears to be weightless. Similarly, water weighed in water displaces its own volume and so is buoyed up by its own weight.

Things you will need:

- balance you made in Experiment 1-3 or electronic or triple-beam balance that can detect hundredths of a gram

- twist-ties

- 2 identical large balloons

- air pump, such as one used to pump bicycle tires or balls used in sports

- football, soccer ball, or other inflatable ball

- needle valve used to inflate balls used in sports

You know that water has mass because you can weigh it in air. The buoyancy effect of the air is much less than the weight of the water. Is there any way to determine the mass of a volume of air?

One way might be to pack more air into a volume than it normally holds. That is, you could increase the air pressure inside a closed container and see if its mass increases. If your balance is quite sensitive, you might be able to detect the weight of air in a balloon. You know that the pressure of the air inside a balloon is greater than the pressure outside because when you release the balloon, the air comes rushing out.

Use twist-ties to hang two large, identical but empty balloons from opposite ends of the balance you built in Experiment 1-3. Use an air pump, such as one used to pump bicycle tires or balls used in sports, to force air into one of the balloons. (Why shouldn't you use air from your lungs in this experiment?) Hang that balloon back on the balance. Can you detect any increase in its mass?

Another approach would be to place an empty balloon and twist-tie on the pan of an electronic or triple-beam balance that can detect hundredths of a gram. Force air into the balloon with an air pump, seal its neck with the twist-tie, and then see if the balloon's mass has increased.

With a football, soccer ball, or any inflatable ball, you can really increase the pressure significantly. You can put two or three times as much air into these volumes as would be there normally. Begin by weighing the ball when no more air will come out of it through a needle valve you stick in the ball. The air inside the ball will then be at the same pressure as the air outside. The ball is now deflated, but not compressed. You should not squeeze the remaining air out because you want the ball's volume to be constant. Remember: An object is buoyed by a force equal to the weight of the fluid (in this case air) it displaces.

Now use the needle valve and air pump to add air to the ball until it is inflated to its recommended pressure or until it feels very firm. Then weigh it again. Can you detect any change in the mass of the ball? If you can, you have succeeded in showing that air has mass.

2-6*
Carbon Dioxide: A Heavier Gas

You may have heard that carbon dioxide gas is used in fire extinguishers because it does not burn, does not support burning, and is heavier than air. Because of its properties, air will "float" on carbon dioxide so that the air will rise above the fire as carbon dioxide buoys it upward. The carbon dioxide will move under the air and smother the fire.

Since carbon dioxide is heavier (more dense) than air, you might be able to see that it has mass by weighing it. To prepare carbon dioxide, you can cause the citric acid and baking soda in seltzer tablets to react with water. The gaseous carbon dioxide that is produced can be collected in a balloon and its mass compared with that of an equal volume of air.

To begin, weigh two identical balloons and twist-ties. If you use the balance you built in Experiment 1-3, you can hang them on opposite ends of the balance beam and adjust the lump of clay until the beam is level.

Next, pour about 25 mL (1 oz) of water into a small, clear flask, like the one shown in Figure 12, or into a small bottle. (An aspirin bottle that holds 250 tablets is satisfactory.) Break two seltzer tablets in half and drop them into the water. Immediately pull the neck of

Things you will need:

- seltzer tablets
- water
- 2 identical balloons
- twist-ties
- balance you built in Experiment 1-3 or another suitable balance
- graduated cylinder or metric measuring cup
- small, clear flask (125–250 mL) or bottle
- paper towel
- bicycle tire pump
- lime water (ask to borrow some from your school's science lab)
- medicine cup
- drinking straw
- 2 identical plastic bags
- short candle
- wide container
- an adult
- matches

a balloon over the top of the bottle or flask. You can see the bubbles of carbon dioxide being released from the water. The gas will fill the balloon and increase its volume as gas continues to be produced by the reaction between the seltzer and water.

Gently swirl the flask or bottle to release as many carbon dioxide bubbles as possible from the water. When the tablets have reacted completely with the water, carefully remove the gas-filled balloon from the flask or bottle. Wipe the mouth of the balloon with a paper towel to be sure it is dry. (Why should the balloon be dry?) Then seal off the balloon with a twist-tie.

Use a bicycle tire pump to fill the second balloon with air. It should have the same volume as the one that is filled with carbon dioxide. Seal its neck with a twist-tie as well. Now hang both balloons

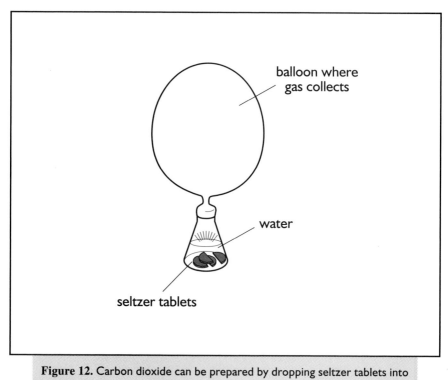

Figure 12. Carbon dioxide can be prepared by dropping seltzer tablets into water.

from opposite ends of the balance. Is the carbon dioxide heavier than air? How do you know?

One way to test for carbon dioxide is to bubble a gas through a solution of lime water (calcium hydroxide dissolved in water). To test the gas in the balloon, place some lime water in a medicine cup. Wrap the neck of the balloon tightly around a drinking straw and carefully remove the twist-tie so that you can bubble the gas into the lime water. If the liquid turns milky, the gas is carbon dioxide. What do you think will happen if you bubble your own breath through lime water? Try it! Were you right?

Generate some more carbon dioxide but collect it in a plastic bag. Fill an identical bag with air. Which one do you think is heavier? Test your prediction. Was it correct?

To see that carbon dioxide can put out fires and is heavier than air, place a short candle in a wide container, as shown in Figure 13. Pour about 50 mL of water around the base of the candle. Then **ask**

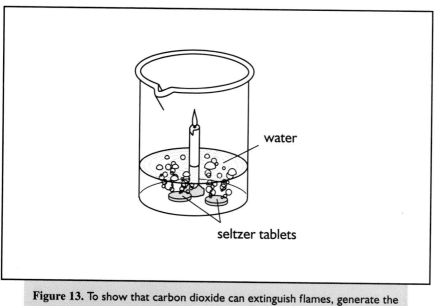

water

seltzer tablets

Figure 13. To show that carbon dioxide can extinguish flames, generate the gas around a burning candle.

an adult to light the candle. After it is burning steadily, generate carbon dioxide by adding two seltzer tablets to the water. Watch the candle closely. What happens? How can you explain what you observe?

Exploring on Your Own

What do you think carbon dioxide would weigh in an atmosphere of carbon dioxide? Design and carry out an experiment that will enable you to make such a weighing.

2-7*
Helium: A Lighter Gas

Obtain a helium-filled balloon. You can find Mylar balloons filled with helium at many variety stores and stores that sell greeting cards.

Things you will need:
- helium-filled balloon
- balance you built in Experiment 1-3 or another suitable balance
- paper clips or other suitable small units of mass

Place the helium-filled balloon on one pan of the balance you built in Experiment 1-3 or another suitable balance. As you can see, helium gas ascends, so it does not push down on the balance. You would have to add weight to the balloon to keep it from floating away. You might say it has negative mass.

To find the apparent negative mass of helium, add paper clips or other units of mass to the helium balloon until the balloon neither rises nor falls in air. What is the apparent negative mass of the helium gas, in grams?

Now remember, you did not take into account the mass of the balloon and any strings or ribbons that may have been attached to it. They were lifted by the helium as well. How can you find the total apparent negative weight of the helium that was in the balloon?

Exploring on Your Own

How much do you think helium would weigh in helium? Design and carry out an experiment to test your prediction.

A helium balloon makes an excellent accelerometer. (An accelerometer is a device that measures changes in velocity.) It will always move horizontally in the direction that it is being accelerated. Take a helium-filled balloon accelerometer on a ride inside an automobile. Sit in the backseat so the driver will not be disturbed. Which way does the balloon move when the car's speed is increasing? When the car's speed is decreasing? When the car goes around a corner? Explain the accelerations indicated by the balloon. Try to explain why the balloon moves as it does when it is accelerated.

2-8*
The Density of Carbon Dioxide Gas

As you have seen, seltzer tablets react with water to form carbon dioxide. If you weigh the water and seltzer before and after the reaction, any loss of mass should be due to the carbon dioxide gas that escapes. By collecting the carbon dioxide, you can measure its volume. Knowing the mass and volume of the gas, you can calculate its density.

To carry out this experiment, break a seltzer tablet in half and place the pieces on the pan of the balance you built in Experiment 1-3. Use a twist-tie to hang a test tube with about 10 mL of water in it from the paper clip to which the pan is attached (see Figure 14a). The test tube should be about ¼ to ⅓ full. Record the combined mass of tablet and test tube.

Next, set up the apparatus shown in Figure 14b. The test tube can be supported by a heavy drinking glass. Fill the large bottle with water and fill the pail about one third of the way with water. Cover the mouth of the bottle with a cardboard square. Hold the square against the bottle as you turn it upside down and put its mouth under the water in the pail. Place the rubber tubing (about 50 cm long) inside and at the top of the large bottle of water. Drop the pieces of tablet into the water in the test

Things you will need:

- seltzer tablet
- balance you built in Experiment 1-3
- twist-tie
- test tube
- graduated cylinder or metric measuring cup
- heavy drinking glass
- water
- pen or pencil
- notebook
- rubber tubing (about 50 cm long)
- one-hole rubber stopper to fit test tube
- glass tube about 10 cm long to fit into rubber stopper
- large bottle (500 mL–1 L [1 pint–1 quart])
- plastic pail
- square piece of cardboard or glass to cover mouth of bottle

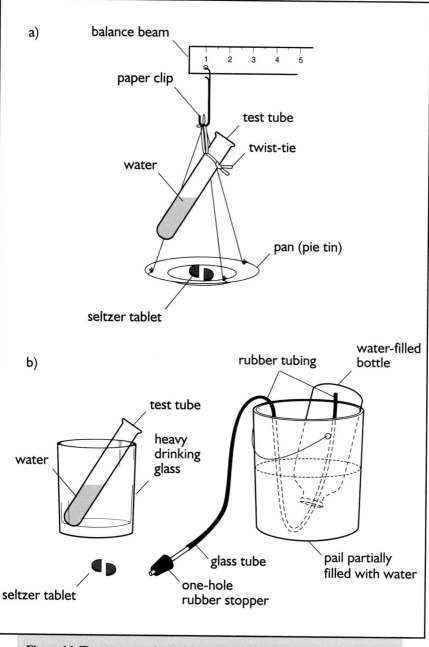

Figure 14. The apparatus shown here, together with a balance and graduated cylinder, will enable you to find the density of carbon dioxide.

tube, then immediately insert a one-hole rubber stopper into the mouth of the test tube. The glass tube and the rubber tubing now connect two containers. Carbon dioxide gas will be produced in the test tube as the tablet reacts with water. The gas will travel through the tubing to the bottle, where it will collect as it displaces water from the bottle.

Let the reaction proceed for about ten minutes. By that time the reaction will be nearly complete.

Remove the rubber tube that extends to the top of the bottle before you remove the rubber stopper from the test tube. Otherwise, air may flow through the tubing into the bottle.

Cover the mouth of the bottle with a square piece of cardboard or glass and remove it from the pail. How can you use a graduated cylinder or metric measuring cup to find the volume of gas that was produced? How can you find the mass of the gas? Record your data in a notebook.

Using the recorded mass and volume of the gas, determine the density of the carbon dioxide. What assumptions have you made in arriving at the density of carbon dioxide?

Exploring on Your Own

Investigate how you might find the density of other gases, using a technique similar to the one you used for carbon dioxide. After you have developed a plan, conduct your experiments **under the supervision of an adult**.

2-9
The Density of Other Gases

This experiment should be done under the supervision of an adult who has experience using a vacuum pump and evacuated containers. He or she may modify this experiment, depending on equipment available.

As you have seen, it is possible to determine whether a gas is more or less dense than air. You can even weigh air if it is under pressure. In the previous experiment, you found a way to measure the density of carbon dioxide. The densities of some other gases can be determined in a similar way; others cannot. In this experiment you will examine the most direct way of finding the density of a gas.

To weigh a volume of air, first determine the volume inside a sturdy metal can. Fill the can with water and then pour the water into a graduated cylinder. What is the volume inside the can?

After the can has been dried, insert a one-hole rubber stopper with a valve into the top of the can. Attach the can to a vacuum pump and **ask the adult** to remove the air from it (see Figure 15a). Once the air has been pumped from the

Things you will need:

- an adult familiar with vacuum pumps and evacuated containers
- sturdy metal can that will hold 250 mL or more
- one-hole rubber stopper to fit can
- 2 small valves
- vacuum pump
- balance you made in Experiment 1-3 or suitable substitute
- pen or pencil
- notebook
- plastic bag (with larger volume than metal can)
- strong rubber bands
- large one-hole rubber stopper
- knife
- short piece of glass tubing
- short length of rubber or plastic tubing
- air pump
- pressurized cylinders of different gases, such as carbon dioxide, oxygen, nitrogen, helium

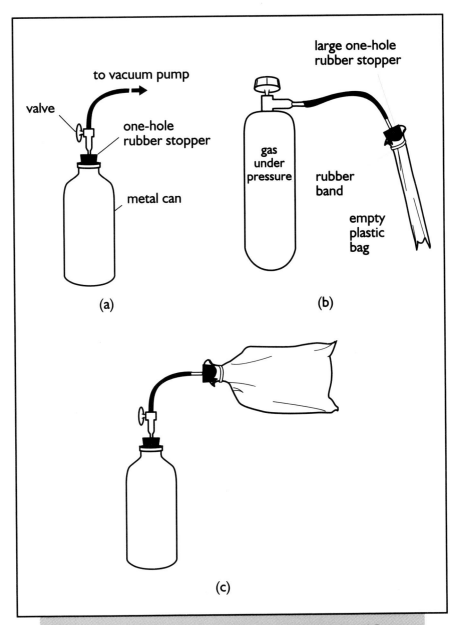

Figure 15. Weighing gases to find their densities can be done by: a) Pumping the air out of a sturdy can and sealing it shut with a valve and weighing the can. b) Filling an empty plastic bag with a gas. c) Connecting the bag of gas to the evacuated can. Then open the valve so gas can flow into the evacuated can. Finally close the valve and reweigh the can.

can, weigh it on a balance. Record the weight. Then open the valve so air can enter the can. Reweigh the can. How can you determine the weight of the air in the can? How can you find the density of the air?

The procedure for weighing other gases is outlined in Figure 15. **Ask the adult** to cut a groove into a one-hole rubber stopper. Then place a glass tube in the hole and attach a short length of rubber or plastic tubing to it. Squeeze all the air from a plastic bag that has a larger volume than the sturdy metal can. Fasten the open end of the bag securely to the rubber stopper with strong rubber bands, as shown in Figure 15b. Then, as is also shown in Figure 15b, connect the bag to a pressurized cylinder of gas that contains carbon dioxide, oxygen, nitrogen, helium, or any other nonpoisonous gas your adult supervisor may provide.

Attach the gas-filled bag to the valve that leads to the can from which the air has been removed (Figure 15c). Open the valve so that air can pass from the bag to the can. When no more gas flows from the bag, close the valve, detach the can, and reweigh it. Record the new mass of the can and gas.

How can you use the data you have collected to determine the mass of the gas? How can you calculate the density of the gas you have weighed?

After you have weighed all the gases available, calculate the mass of each gas by subtracting the mass of the evacuated can from the mass of the gas-filled can. What was the mass of each gas? How do their densities compare? What must you do to find the actual densities, in g/cm^3, of the gases you weighed?

There is a less direct way to find the density of gases. You must know the density of air and the volume of the gas-filled plastic bag. The density of air at room temperature (20 °C or 68 °F) and atmospheric pressure (760 torr or 100,000 Pa) is approximately 1.2 grams per liter (g/L).

Weighing the bag when it is filled with air will give you the weight of the bag and any attachments. The air will be buoyed up by a force equal to its own weight.

From Experiment 1-2, you know how to find the volume of the gas in the bag by squeezing it out so that the volume of water it displaces can be measured.

Suppose the volume of gas in the bag is 800 mL. Then you know the mass of the air in the bag is:

$$1.2 \text{ g/L} \times 0.80 \text{ L} = 0.96 \text{ g.}$$

You can then weigh the bag when it is filled with another gas. The bag of gas will be buoyed up by the weight of the air displaced. After subtracting the weight of the bag and attachments, you should add 0.96 g, or whatever you find the mass of the air to be, to the mass of each gas you weigh to find the actual mass of the gas in the bag of known volume.

What is the mass and density of each gas?

3

Making Solids and Liquids Disappear and Reappear

Although solids and liquids are clearly visible, they can be made to disappear. They can also be made to reappear. In some cases, a solid disappears and a liquid appears, or a liquid disappears and a solid appears. The change of a substance from solid to liquid, liquid to solid, liquid to gas, gas to liquid, and so on, is known as a change of state.

3-1*
Making Solids Disappear

Use a graduated cylinder or metric measuring cup to pour 100 mL of room-temperature water into each of two glasses. Add a level teaspoonful of sugar to one of the glasses of water and stir the mixture. What happens to the solid sugar?

Repeat the experiment using a level teaspoonful of kosher salt. (Kosher salt is recommended because it does not have added substances that make water cloudy.) Stir the mixture. What happens to the salt?

When solids disappear in liquids, we say that a solute (solid) has dissolved in a solvent (liquid) to form a solution. Use a teaspoon to remove a tiny bit of liquid from the sugar solution. Place the liquid on your tongue. Can you taste the dissolved sugar?

Repeat the experiment with the salt solution. Can you taste the dissolved salt?

Things you will need:

- graduated cylinder or metric measuring cup
- room-temperature water
- glasses
- teaspoon
- sugar
- salt (kosher salt if possible)
- coffee filters
- funnel
- other solids such as baking soda, Epsom salts, flavored crystals, flour, and cornstarch
- other liquids such as rubbing alcohol, vinegar, and cooking oil
- dry ice (see telephone book for a source)
- heavy gloves
- an adult
- flask or small bottle like the one used to produce carbon dioxide in Experiment 2-5
- balloon
- balance
- iodine crystals
- fume hood
- science teacher

Perhaps you can separate the solute from the solvent by pouring the solution through a filter. Fold a coffee filter to make a conical filter, as shown in Figure 16. (Note: If you use a #2 or #4 filter, you do not have to fold it to fit the funnel.) Place the filter in

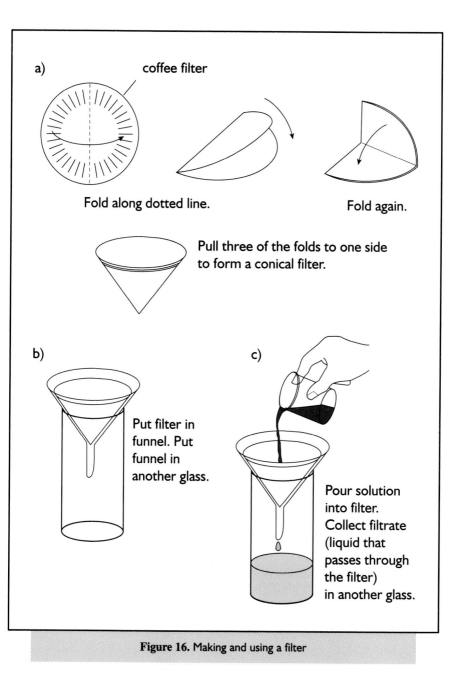

a)

coffee filter

Fold along dotted line.

Fold again.

Pull three of the folds to one side to form a conical filter.

b)

Put filter in funnel. Put funnel in another glass.

c)

Pour solution into filter. Collect filtrate (liquid that passes through the filter) in another glass.

Figure 16. Making and using a filter

a funnel. Pour some of the sugar solution into the filter and collect the liquid that comes through in a small glass. After all the liquid has flowed through the filter, can you see any sugar on the filter paper? Can you still taste sugar in the liquid that came through the filter paper?

Do you think you can separate salt from the water in which it dissolved by pouring it through a filter? Try it! Were you right?

Add 100 mL of sugar to 100 mL of water and stir. Do you get 200 mL of solution? Can you explain the results you obtain?

Solids that dissolve are said to be soluble. Solids that do not dissolve are said to be insoluble. Sugar and salt are soluble in water. What other substances are soluble in water? You might try baking soda (sodium bicarbonate), Epsom salts (magnesium sulfate), flavored crystals, flour, and cornstarch. Which of these solids are soluble in water? Are there any that are insoluble?

Remember, do not put any materials in your mouth unless directed to do so.

Can other liquids serve as solvents? Try to dissolve solids that were soluble in water in rubbing alcohol, vinegar, and cooking oil. In which solvents are the solutes soluble? What happens when baking soda is added to vinegar? Can you explain why it happens?

Sublimation

Another way that solids sometimes disappear is sublimation. Solids whose atoms or molecules are not strongly attracted to one another will change from solid to gas without passing through a liquid stage.

If possible, obtain a piece of dry ice. **Ask an adult to help you because dry ice is very cold (−78.5 °C or −109 °F) and should always be handled while wearing heavy gloves.** Place a small piece of dry ice in a flask or small bottle as you did when you made carbon dioxide in Experiment 2-5. Collect the gas in a balloon as you did in that experiment. Does it weigh more than air?

Iodine crystals will also sublimate. If your school has a fume hood, ask your science teacher to help you gently heat a few iodine crystals in a beaker. **All the apparatus should be in a fume hood that will draw away any vapors so that you do not come in contact with the iodine fumes.** What is the color of gaseous iodine?

Exploring on Your Own

A saturated solution is one that will hold no more solid. Design and carry out experiments to find out how much salt is required to make a saturated solution in 100 mL of room-temperature water. How much sugar is required to make a saturated solution in 100 mL of water?

Will twice as much solvent dissolve twice as much salt or sugar? Design and carry out experiments to find out.

Design and carry out experiments to find out whether temperature affects the mass of salt that will dissolve in a fixed volume of water. Does it affect the mass of sugar that will dissolve in a fixed volume of water?

Investigate the ways in which solubility can be used to help identify solids.

Investigate the use of iodine vapor in forensic science as a way of making fingerprints visible.

Investigate solutions made by dissolving gas in liquids. How are these solutions affected by temperature and pressure?

3-2*
Making Solids Reappear

As you saw in the previous experiment, solids disappear when they dissolve in a solvent. They do not reappear if you pour the solution through a filter. Is there any way to make the solids reappear?

One approach might be to let the solution evaporate. Will the solution, both solute and solvent, evaporate, or will the solvent evaporate, leaving the solute behind? To find out, using water as a solvent, prepare separate sat-

Things you will need:

- salt, sugar, Epsom salts (magnesium sulfate), and alum (potassium aluminum sulfate) (alum can be obtained at a pharmacy or your school's science lab)
- teaspoons
- metric measuring cup
- water
- glasses
- saucers
- paper and pencil to make labels
- magnifying glass
- hot water

urated solutions of salt, sugar, Epsom salts, and alum. A saturated solution is one in which as much solute as possible has dissolved. To prepare a saturated alum solution, add the solute (alum) in teaspoonful quantities to 100 mL of water in a glass. After each teaspoonful, stir with a different teaspoon until all of the solid has dissolved or until no more will dissolve. Prepare saturated solutions of salt, sugar, and Epsom salts in the same way. Label each solution so that it can be identified. Leave these solutions overnight to be sure that as much solute as possible has dissolved.

On the next day, pour only the solutions into separate saucers, leaving any solid behind. Again place labels beside the saucers so the solutions can be identified. Leave the solutions for several days. Check them periodically. What do you find happening? Do both solute and solvent evaporate, or does just the solvent evaporate? How can you tell?

When the solids are thoroughly dry, use a magnifying glass to look closely at the dry solids that remain. You should be able to see small particles with a characteristic shape on each saucer. These particles are crystals. How do the shapes of the crystals on any one saucer compare? How do the shapes of the crystals on different saucers compare?

Which crystals are cubic? Which crystals have a long needle-like shape? Which crystals have hexagonal-shaped faces?

Do you like rock candy? You can make some quite easily. Add a cup of sugar to half a cup of hot water. Stir and let stand for a few days. This is one experiment you **can** eat.

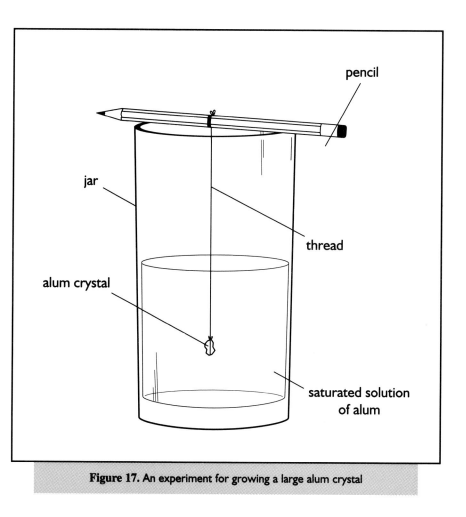

Figure 17. An experiment for growing a large alum crystal

Exploring on Your Own

Why do you think you were asked to pour the solutions onto saucers? To check on your explanation, pour 100 mL of water into a glass. Pour another 100 mL of water onto a saucer. Place both in a warm place. What do you conclude?

With patience, you can prepare beautiful, large crystals of alum. Prepare a saturated alum solution as before and let it stand overnight to be sure it is saturated. Pour some or all of the solution into a wide-mouth jar. Using forceps, pick up one of the crystals from the saucer of alum crystals you prepared. Have someone hold the crystal with the forceps while you attach it to a thread, using a slip knot. This will take patience because the crystal is small and delicate.

Once you have the crystal on a string, tie the other end of the thread to a pencil. Lay the pencil across the top of the jar so that the crystal is submerged in the saturated alum solution, as shown in Figure 17. The crystal will grow slowly. If the crystal dissolves, you will know that the solution was not saturated.

If you succeed in growing a large crystal of alum, you may want to grow your own collection of "gems." Find some books on crystal growing and grow crystals patiently in your "gem garden."

3-3*
Making Liquids Disappear

You already know how to make solvents disappear—you let them evaporate. Will a pure solvent evaporate faster than one to which solute has been added?

To find out, prepare a saturated salt solution. Pour 25 mL of the salt solution onto a saucer. Pour 25 mL of water onto an identical saucer. Leave both saucers side by side in the same place. Observe the two liquids periodically. What do you conclude?

Things you will need:
- saturated salt solution
- graduated cylinder or metric measuring cup
- saucers
- water
- 2 identical cooking pans
- an adult
- stove
- rubbing alcohol
- cooking oil

You can make a liquid disappear much faster by heating it. Pour 100 mL of water into each of two identical cooking pans. **Under adult supervision**, heat one pan on a stove. Leave the other pan nearby but do not heat it. From which pan does water disappear faster?

Does one kind of solvent disappear (evaporate) faster than another? You can find out by placing 20 grams of water, rubbing alcohol, and cooking oil on identical saucers. Place all three saucers in the same place. **(Do not heat them.)** Do the three liquids disappear at the same rate? If not, which liquid disappears fastest? Which disappears slowest?

Exploring on Your Own

Why were you asked to place equal masses rather than equal volumes of the solvents on identical saucers?

3-4*
Making a Liquid Reappear (and a Gas Appear)

There is a very simple way to make a liquid reappear and a gas appear. It involves boiling the water and then condensing it.

A liquid's boiling point is the temperature at which it changes to a gas. The bubbles of gas that form in the heated liquid no longer collapse. They rise to the surface and escape as a gas.

The change of a gas to a liquid is called condensation. The condensation point of a gaseous substance is the same temperature as the substance's boiling point. If heat is being added, it boils. If heat is being removed, it condenses.

Things you will need:
- teakettle
- water
- stove
- heavy gloves
- an adult
- drinking glass
- cold water
- ice
- shiny metal can

To make a liquid reappear and a gas appear, place a teakettle containing water on a stove. **Under adult supervision**, turn on the burner. When the water boils, you will see steam coming from the spout of the teakettle. Actually, what most people call steam is really gaseous water that has condensed to tiny droplets of liquid water. If you look closely, you will see a clear region just above the spout. That is where the gaseous water is found.

To change the invisible gas above the spout into liquid water, you will need to first put on a pair of heavy gloves. Then, **under adult supervision**, hold the bottom of a cold glass of water in the clear gas at the mouth of the teakettle's spout. What do you find collecting and falling from the bottom of the glass? What liquid reappeared? What gas was changed so that it became visible as a liquid?

During warm seasons, especially in the summer, you can make liquids appear just as dew appears on grass after a clear summer night.

Fill a shiny metal can with ice. Add water and watch the surface of the can. If the humidity is high, droplets of water will begin to appear on the can's surface. Where do you think they came from?

Exploring on Your Own

One possible explanation for the formation of water droplets on the surface of a can of cold water is that water is leaking through the can. Design an experiment to show that water is not leaking through the can.

Investigate the meaning of *dew point*. Then design an experiment to measure the dew point in the room where you found water appearing on the surface of the shiny can of cold water.

3-5
Temperature and Making Liquids Disappear

Because you will be using a stove and hot materials in this experiment, you should work under the supervision of an adult. You should also wear safety glasses throughout the experiment.

Turn on one of the small heating elements on a stove. Half-fill a cooking pan with cold water and place a laboratory thermometer that has a scale from –10 °C to 110 °C in the pan, as shown in Figure 18. What is the temperature of the cold water? Next, put the pan of water with the thermometer in it on the stove's heating element.

As the water is being heated, record the water temperature every minute. Also watch what happens in the water. You will see small bubbles form and rise to the surface. Some of these bubbles are due to air that was dissolved in the water. You may have noticed similar bubbles that form when a cold glass of water is left out overnight. Some of the bubbles result from liquid water changing to gas. When the water begins to boil, the bubbles of water vapor rise vigorously to the surface and burst. What do you notice about the temperature of the water when it begins to boil vigorously?

Continue heating the water until about half of it has changed to a gas. Continue to record the water temperature during this time. What is the temperature? Does it change?

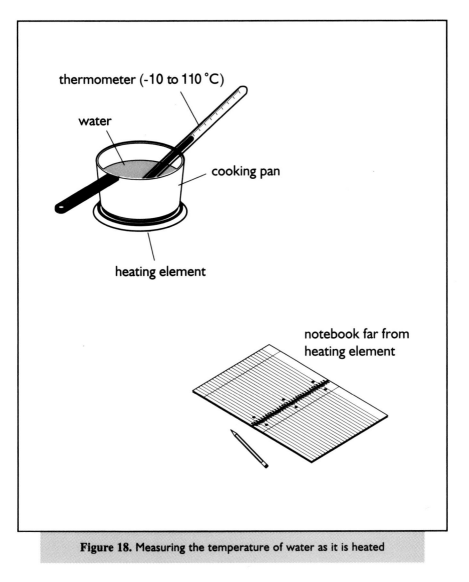

thermometer (-10 to 110 °C)

water

cooking pan

heating element

notebook far from
heating element

Figure 18. Measuring the temperature of water as it is heated

Plot a graph of your data. Make temperature the vertical (y) axis of your graph and time the horizontal (x) axis. How can you explain the shape of the graph you have plotted?

A Test of Another Substance

DO NOT TRY THIS EXPERIMENT. Using precautions to avoid its flammability, the author heated a small volume of ethyl alcohol to boiling, recorded its temperature over a period of time, and plotted a graph of the data. The graph is shown in Figure 19. What do you conclude about the temperature at which ethyl alcohol boils?

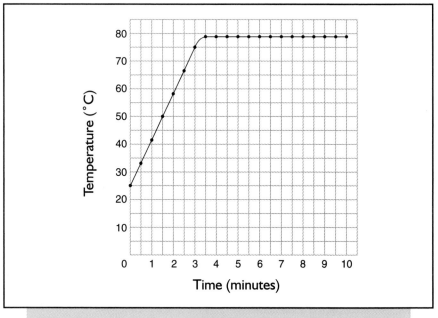

Figure 19. A temperature vs. time graph shows what happens to a small sample of ethyl alcohol when it is heated.

3-6*
Making Solids Disappear as Liquids Appear and Vice Versa

Things you will need:

- chopped ice or snow
- large Styrofoam cup (12 oz)
- thermometer with scale that extends to 0 °C (32 °F) and below
- plastic pail
- water
- small Styrofoam cup (7 oz)
- scissors
- pen or pencil
- notebook
- freezer
- clock or watch
- graph paper

Put a handful of chopped ice or snow in a large Styrofoam cup. Use a thermometer that can measure temperatures down to and below 0 °C (32 °F) to stir the ice or snow. What is the lowest temperature the ice or snow reaches as you stir it? Continue stirring the cold solid for several minutes. Does the temperature change or does it remain about the same? At what temperature does ice or snow melt according to your thermometer?

Repeat the experiment with a plastic pail half-filled with chopped ice or snow. Does the mass of the ice or snow affect the temperature at which it melts?

Pour about 50 mL of water into a small Styrofoam cup. Place a thermometer that can measure temperatures down to and below 0 °C (32 °F) in the water. If necessary, use scissors to cut away part of the side of the cup so that you can see the thermometer scale clearly.

Record the temperature of the water in your notebook. Then put the cup with the water and thermometer in a freezer where you can read the thermometer by simply opening the freezer door. Continue to record the temperature of the water every ten minutes until the temperature reaches its lowest point. What happens to the tempera-ture while the water is freezing? What happens to the temperature after the water is frozen? Why does the temperature finally reach a minimum?

Leave the frozen water and thermometer in the freezer overnight. On the next day, remove the frozen water from the freezer. Record its temperature at ten-minute intervals until it reaches room temperature.

Using the data you have collected, plot graphs of temperature versus time for the water as it cooled and froze and for the ice as it melted and warmed. You can plot both graphs on the same set of axes.

How does the graph of the water cooling and solidifying compare with the graph of the ice melting and warming to room temperature?

Exploring on Your Own

Under adult supervision, place a test tube that is nearly filled with acetamide crystals in a beaker of hot water. (You can probably obtain acetamide from your science teacher or a science supply house [see appendix] through your school.) Heat the water to about 90 °C and keep the temperature at that level until all the acetamide melts. Use a test tube clamp to remove the test tube with the melted acetamide from the hot water. Fasten the test tube containing the acetamide to a ring stand. Hang a thermometer from the same ring stand so that its bulb is near the center of the liquid acetamide.

Record the temperature at 30-second intervals until the acetamide crystals reach a temperature close to that of the room. What do you find the freezing temperature of acetamide to be? What would you expect its melting temperature to be? Design and, **under adult supervision**, carry out an experiment to find the melting temperature of acetamide.

Boiling, Freezing, Melting, and Condensing Points (Temperatures)

Substances boil or condense at different temperatures; they also melt or freeze at different temperatures. The temperature at which a substance boils (its boiling point) is a characteristic property. Boiling points and melting points are often used to help identify an unknown substance. The boiling, melting, freezing, and condensing points of a few common substances are shown in Table 1. How do the freezing and melting points compare? How do the boiling and condensing points compare?

Which of the substances listed in Table 1 would be liquids at room temperature (25 °C or 77 °F)? Which would be gases? Which would be solids?

Table 1: Boiling, condensing, melting, and freezing points of some common substances

Substance	Boiling Point (°C)	Condensing Point (°C)	Melting Point (°C)	Freezing Point (°C)
aluminum	1,800	1,800	658	658
lead	1,525	1,525	327	327
salt	1,413	1,413	801	801
mercury	357	357	−39	−39
naphthalene	218	218	80	80
water	100	100	0	0
ethyl alcohol	78	78	−117	−117
methyl alcohol	65	65	−98	−98
oxygen	−184	−184	−219	−219
nitrogen	−195	−195	−210	−210
hydrogen	−253	− 253	−259	−259
helium	−268	−268	−271	−271

3-7*
Making a Liquid Appear in a Chemical Reaction

Because you will be using matches and a flame, this experiment should be done under adult supervision.

Chill a large, widemouthed glass bottle in the refrigerator for about ten minutes. Place a candle in a candleholder and light the candle. When the candle is burning well, hold the cold bottle above the flame, as shown in Figure 20. After several minutes, you should begin to see a thin film of liquid collecting on the sides of the jar. The liquid is water.

Things you will need:

- an adult
- large, widemouthed glass bottle
- refrigerator
- candle
- candleholder
- matches

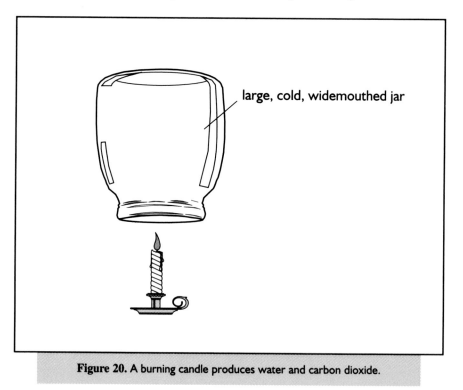

large, cold, widemouthed jar

Figure 20. A burning candle produces water and carbon dioxide.

It is one of the products produced when candle wax burns. The other product (unseen) is carbon dioxide.

The reaction is summarized by the chemical equation:

$$\text{candle wax} + O_2 \rightarrow H_2O + CO_2.$$

The reaction is a chemical change because new substances are formed. You started with candle wax and the oxygen in air. These two chemicals combined to form water and carbon dioxide. Because the temperature was above water's boiling point, water was produced in the gaseous state. When the gas struck the cold glass, it condensed to liquid water. Based on the fact that water and carbon dioxide were produced when candle wax combined chemically with oxygen, what elements must be present in candle wax?

Exploring on Your Own

Explain why water was evident as a product of this reaction but carbon dioxide was not.

Investigate how water and carbon dioxide can be identified. Then design and, **under adult supervision**, carry out an experiment to show that the gases produced when a candle burns really are water and carbon dioxide.

Liquids Disappearing in Other Liquids

Sometimes, when you add one liquid to another, they mingle and there is no way to distinguish one from the other. Such liquids are said to be miscible; they dissolve in one another. In other cases, the liquids remain separate and distinct; we say they are immiscible. In still other cases, liquids that are miscible can be distinguished from one another and remain separated for some time because of differences in density.

Things you will need:

- clear glasses
- rubbing alcohol
- water
- cooking oil
- salt (kosher if possible)
- food coloring
- clear plastic vial or medicine cup
- eyedropper
- quiet place where liquids will not be disturbed

Pour a few milliliters of rubbing alcohol into a few milliliters of water. What happens? Would you say that alcohol and water are miscible or immiscible?

Pour a few milliliters of cooking oil into a few milliliters of water. What happens? Would you say that cooking oil and water are miscible or immiscible?

Prepare a saturated salt solution (see Experiment 3-2). Pour a few milliliters of the solution into a few milliliters of water. What happens? Would you say that the salt solution and water are miscible or immiscible?

Add a few drops of food coloring to the salt solution to make it more visible. Next, half-fill a clear plastic vial or medicine cup with water. Now, use an eyedropper to very slowly and carefully place a layer of the colored salt solution underneath the water in the vial or medicine cup. You can do this by very slowly squeezing the salt solution from the eyedropper beneath the water and onto the bottom of the vessel, as shown in Figure 21. Can a saturated salt

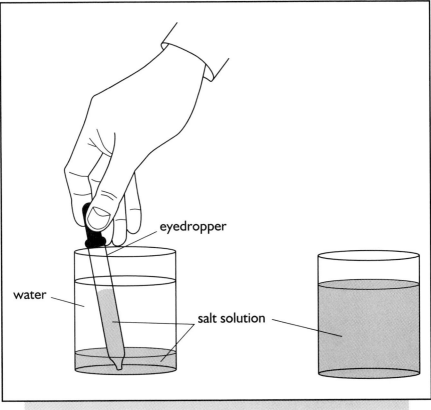

Figure 21. Place a layer of salt solution beneath the water in a vial.

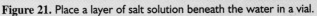

solution and water be placed in separate layers, even though they are miscible?

Leave the layered water and colored salt solution in a quiet place for several days or weeks. What happens to the two layers as time passes?

3-9*
Diffusion

If molecules are in constant motion, you would expect them to spread out, to move through space. The spreading out of molecules through space because they move is called *diffusion*. Of course, the atoms or molecules in solids can only vibrate in place; they are not free to move about one another the way liquid molecules do. In general, therefore, solids do not diffuse. Layers of rocks that have been in contact for millions of years still reveal sharp boundaries. Nevertheless, because of holes (vacancies) in crystals, some solids do diffuse very slowly into other solids.

Diffusion of Liquids

You might expect liquids to diffuse more rapidly because their molecules are free to move about one another. To see if you can observe diffusion in liquids, add a drop of food coloring to a glass of cold water. Watch the colored drop closely. What happens? Can you detect evidence of diffusion?

Things you will need:
- food coloring
- drinking glasses
- cold water
- hot water
- hydrated copper sulfate ($CuSO_4 \cdot H_2O$)
- small beaker or measuring cup
- graduated cylinder or metric measuring cup
- distilled water
- test tube
- support to keep test tube upright
- eyedropper
- rubber or plastic tubing
- small funnel
- a friend
- bottle of perfume or household ammonia
- ruler
- science teacher
- rubber gloves
- ammonium hydroxide (NH_4OH)
- concentrated hydrochloric acid (HCl)
- watch or clock
- pen or pencil
- notebook
- tape measure

Based on the molecular model of matter you read about in Chapter 1, how would you expect the rate of diffusion to be affected by temperature?

To test your prediction, place a glass of hot water and a glass of cold water side by side. Be sure there are no gas bubbles or currents in the water. Then add a drop of food coloring to each liquid. Can you see any difference in the rate at which the food coloring diffuses through the water? How long does it take before the color is uniformly spread in each glass? Does temperature affect the rate of diffusion?

The density of food coloring is very close to the density of water. What will happen if you place a denser liquid beneath a less dense one? Will diffusion still occur? Or will gravity be able to overcome upward molecular motion?

To find out, add 4 grams of hydrated copper sulfate ($CuSO_4 \cdot H_2O$) to a small beaker or measuring cup. Add 15 mL of distilled water and stir until all the blue crystals dissolve. Next, add distilled water to a test tube until it is about half filled. Support the test tube in an upright position in a place where it will not be disturbed.

To place the blue copper sulfate solution beneath the water in the test tube, you will need an eyedropper (but not the rubber bulb), a length of rubber or plastic tubing, and a small funnel. Attach one end of the tubing to the wide end of the eyedropper and the other end to the funnel, as shown in Figure 22a. Put the end of the eyedropper on the bottom of the test tube. Hold the funnel with one hand and keep the thumb and index finger of your other hand on the tubing so that you can control the flow of liquid through it. Ask a friend to pour the blue solution into the funnel. Then let the solution flow very slowly onto the bottom of the tube beneath the clear water.

After all the liquid has reached the test tube, you will have a blue layer of liquid beneath a clear layer, as seen in Figure 22b. Why

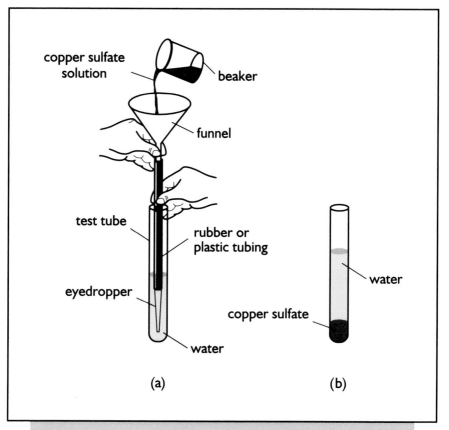

Figure 22. a) The diagram shows how a layer of copper sulfate can be placed under a layer of water. b) Two distinct layers are shown in a test tube.

do you think the blue layer of copper sulfate remains under the clear layer of water?

Watch the layers in the tube over the next several weeks. Do you see any evidence of diffusion? If you do, how long does it take before the tube has a uniform color?

Diffusion of Gases

You might expect gases to diffuse more rapidly than liquids because the molecules are farther apart. On the other hand, there are fewer of them in a given volume, and if released into air they will bump into the air molecules as they move.

One way to look for the diffusion of gases is to open a bottle of perfume or household ammonia. Stand several meters from the bottle, record the time, and wait. How long does it take before your sense of smell tells you that the gas molecules of perfume or ammonia have reached you?

Measure the distance between you and the bottle. Use the distance and time to determine the average speed of the molecules. These molecules are actually moving at more than 100 meters per second. Why did it take so long for them to travel the short distance between you and the bottle from which they came?

Ask your science teacher to help you with another experiment to show that gases diffuse. Place a bottle of ammonium hydroxide (NH_4OH) about one meter away from a bottle of concentrated hydrochloric acid (HCl). Wearing rubber gloves, use one hand to remove the glass stopper from the bottle of hydrochloric acid. With your other hand, remove the stopper from the bottle that holds ammonium hydroxide. Keeping the two stoppers about half a meter apart, give the gaseous fumes from the two solutions time to diffuse (see Figure 23). If they diffuse far enough from the stoppers to meet, you will see a white cloud form. The cloud is ammonium chloride, a white solid that forms when hydrogen chloride (HCl) gas, which comes from the hydrochloric acid, and ammonia gas, which comes from the ammonium hydroxide, combine. The formula for the reaction is:

$$HCl + NH_3 \rightarrow NH_4Cl.$$

Does a white cloud form? How were the reactants (HCl and NH_3), which were half a meter apart, able to combine to form the product (NH_4Cl)?

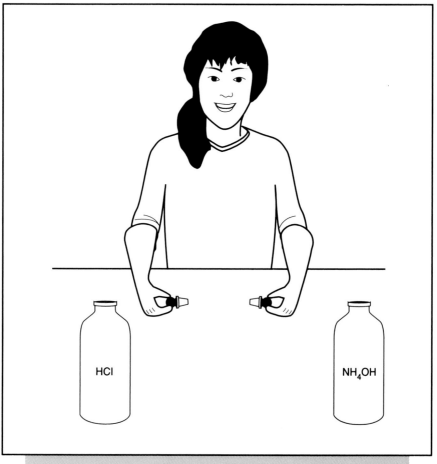

Figure 23. An experiment to see if hydrogen chloride and ammonia will diffuse and form a white cloud of ammonium chloride

Exploring on Your Own

Design an experiment that will allow you to make an estimate of the relative molecular speeds of ammonia and hydrogen chloride. **With the help of your science teacher**, carry out the experiment. What do you find their relative molecular speeds to be?

4

Liquid Surface Tension and Viscosity

If you have ever watched a drop of water hang from the end of a faucet, you know that water has a tendency to hang together with itself. Such a tendency must affect the attraction of water molecules for one another. Because water molecules attract one another so strongly, the surface of water behaves as if it has a skin. Some insects can walk on the water's skin. You may have noticed the tiny dimples in the water that is stretched beneath their feet.

The strong attraction of molecules, such as water molecules, for one another is a characteristic property known as surface tension. In the next three experiments, you will see its effects and how it can be measured. Then you will turn your attention from the "stickiness" of water to its "thickness" or viscosity and try to determine if thickness is related to density.

4-1
Heaping Liquids

Fill a clean, thoroughly-rinsed medicine cup or plastic vial with water. You may think the vessel is full, but because of water's surface tension it can hold more. To see that this is true, use a clean, thoroughly rinsed eyedropper to add drops of water to the container. After the water is level with the top of the cup or vial, how many drops of water can you add before water finally runs down the sides?

From a bottle of liquid detergent, carefully squeeze a single drop of the detergent onto the

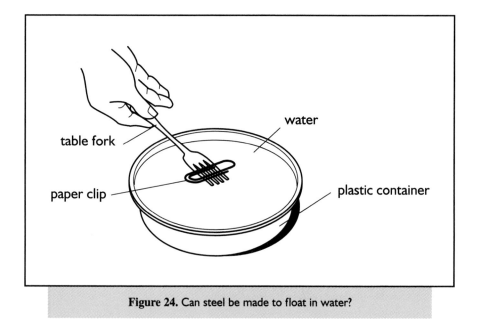

Figure 24. Can steel be made to float in water?

water heaped above the cup or vial. What happens? What does this tell you about the surface tension of soapy water?

Using a clean, thoroughly rinsed medicine cup or plastic vial and an eyedropper, see how high you can heap rubbing alcohol. Does alcohol appear to have more or less surface tension than water?

Pour some water into a clean, wide, thoroughly rinsed plastic container, such as the kind that frozen whipped toppings come in. Use a clean table fork to gently place a paper clip on the water's surface, as shown in Figure 24. Is the water's surface dimpled as it is when insects stride on it?

Predict what will happen if you add a drop of liquid detergent to the water. Try it! Were you right?

4-2*
Climbing Liquids

Because water holds together so well, it can actually pull itself up inside narrow tubes. To do this, the molecules at the top of the water column must adhere to the tube's surface and support the weight of the water below.

One material that has narrow "tubes" within it is paper. To see these tubes, tear off a piece of paper towel or blotter paper and examine it with a magnifying glass or microscope. You will see tiny wood fibers that are packed together very closely. The closely packed fibers have narrow spaces between them that behave as if they were narrow tubes. If you place the edge of the paper against a few drops of water on the edge of a kitchen sink or a microscope slide, you can watch through your magnifier or microscope and see the water move between the fibers.

To see how the width of a narrow opening affects the upward movement of water, add some water to a pie tin. Color the water with a few drops of food coloring to make it more visible. Then place two drinking glasses with straight sides in the water. Bring the sides of the glasses very close together, as shown in Figure 25a. What happens to the level of the water between the two glasses as the space between them decreases?

Things you will need:

- paper towels or blotter paper
- magnifying glass or microscope
- kitchen sink or a microscope slide
- water
- pie tin
- food coloring
- 2 drinking glasses with straight sides
- shallow container
- 2 plates of flat glass such as window panes
- heavy gloves
- pencil
- scissors
- tape
- plastic tube or waxed paper

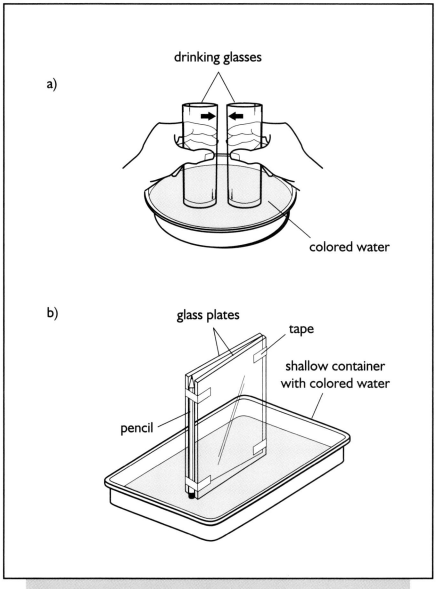

a) drinking glasses

colored water

b) glass plates

tape

shallow container
with colored water

pencil

Figure 25. Experiments show the effect of tube width on the rise of water.

A still better way to see the effect of the width of a space on the rise of water is with two plates of flat glass, such as window panes. To avoid cutting your hands, **wear heavy gloves**. Put a pencil between the plates at one end. Then tape the plates together at both ends to make a thin wedge-shaped space between them. Put the plates in a container of shallow colored water, as shown in Figure 25b. How does this experiment show the effect of tube width on the height to which water will rise?

To see how water will climb to greater heights, cut a strip of paper towel or (better) blotter paper that is about 40 cm long and 2 cm wide. Use tape to hang the strip so that one end dips into a shallow container of water to which you have added a few drops of food coloring. The color will help you to see the water as it rises in the paper or blotter. Can you see the water "climb" up the paper?

Check the paper periodically over the next few hours. What is the maximum height to which the water rises? Why do you think it stops rising?

Perhaps the size of the spaces between the wood fibers prevents the water from rising higher. On the other hand, perhaps the water evaporates from the paper. When the rate of evaporation equals the rate at which water enters the paper, the water stops rising because none remains at the top of the column.

You can do an experiment to see what effect, if any, evaporation has on the rise of water in the paper or blotter. Repeat the first experiment, using two identical lengths of blotter paper or paper towel. Cover one of the strips with a plastic tube or a piece of waxed paper that is rolled into a tube and taped shut along its side. Seal the top of the plastic or waxed paper tube with tape. Leave the bottom of the tube open so the paper can dip into the colored water. Leave both strips of paper or blotter with their lower ends in water overnight. Does the water rise higher in the paper that is covered? If it does, can you explain why it does?

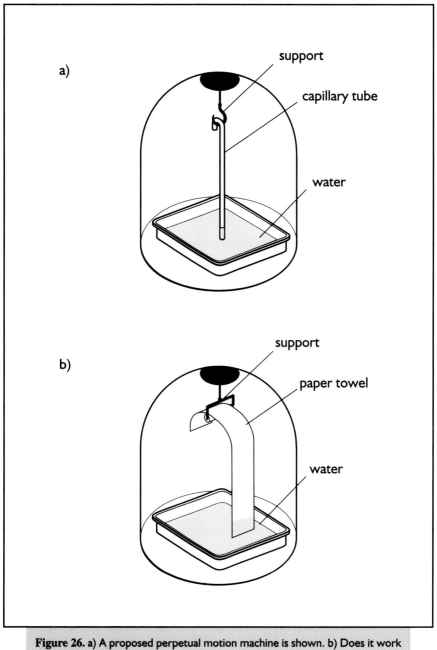

Figure 26. a) A proposed perpetual motion machine is shown. b) Does it work with a working model?

Exploring on Your Own

Try placing identical strips of paper towel or blotter in different liquids. You can use water as your standard and compare it with such liquids as rubbing alcohol, cooking oil, vinegar, saltwater, and soapy water. Do different liquids ascend to the same or different heights?

Does the width of the paper or blotter strip have any effect on the height to which water will rise? If it does, how can you explain the results?

A man once thought he could build a perpetual motion machine by suspending a bent piece of very narrow (capillary) tubing in a covered container of water, as shown in Figure 26a. He argued that water would rise in the tube, fall out the end, and return to rise up the tube again.

Do you think such a device will work? You can build such a "machine" by using a length of paper towel, as shown in Figure 26b. Does it work as the man proposed? Can anyone ever build a perpetual motion machine?

Show how you can use a paper towel to siphon water.

4-3*
Measuring Surface Tension

To measure how well liquids hold together, which is what causes surface tension, you can use the balance you built in Experiment 1-3. The balance can be used to measure the force needed to pull liquids apart.

Using scissors, cut a square that is 4 cm on a side from a piece of plastic. You can cut the squares from the plastic tops that come with coffee cans or margarine tubs. **Ask an adult to help you** use pliers to push a heated common pin through the center of each square. Use the same pliers to bend the end of the pin. When you finish, the square and pin should look like the model shown in Figure 27a.

To measure the force needed to pull liquids apart, the plastic

Things you will need:
- balance you built in Experiment 1-3
- scissors
- flat pieces of plastic, such as the plastic tops that come with coffee cans or margarine tubs
- an adult
- pliers
- common pins
- matches
- water
- thread
- paper clips
- dish to hold shallow layer of water
- small box or pieces of cardboard
- rubbing alcohol
- soapy water

square must adhere (stick) to the water more strongly than the water coheres (holds together). To be certain this is the case with the plastic you are using, hang the square you made from a piece of thread. Then lower the plastic onto the surface of some water. Slowly raise the plastic off the water's surface. Look on the bottom of the square. Is there water on the surface of the plastic? If there is, the water must have been pulled apart.

If there is no water on the square, the force holding the water to the square (adhesion) was less than the forces holding the water

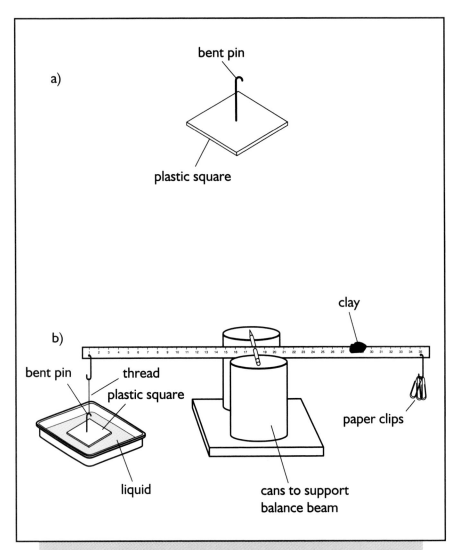

Figure 27. a) A plastic square with a bent pin that can be used to lift the square. b) An experiment to measure surface tension, or how well different liquids hold together (cohere).

together (cohesion). If this is the case, you will need to find a different plastic—one that adheres more strongly to water.

Once you have found a plastic that adheres strongly to water, use thread to hang the plastic square from one end of the balance beam (by convention, unknown masses are placed on the left-hand side of a balance). Add paper clips or move the clay on the beam until the beam is level. Next, put a shallow dish of water under the square. If necessary, use a small box or pieces of cardboard to raise the dish until the water touches the plastic square.

To measure the force needed to pull the plastic off the water, carefully add paper clips to the opposite end of the beam, as shown in Figure 27b. If you look closely at the place where water and plastic touch, you can see that the water adhering to the plastic is being lifted by the force produced by adding the paper clips. The force is stretching the water's surface and lifting a small volume of water. Try to estimate the volume of water that is lifted before the water breaks apart.

Repeat the experiment, using different liquids, including rubbing alcohol, soapy water, and cooking oil. Be sure to thoroughly clean the plate before changing liquids. Do the results agree with what you might expect from Experiments 4-1 and 4-2?

Exploring on Your Own

How does the surface area of the plastic pieces affect the force needed to pull them off the water? To find out, make additional squares with different areas. **Under adult supervision**, add pins so that the squares can be hung from the balance beam. Then carry out your experiment. What do you find?

Prepare other plastic pieces with different shapes—a circle, a rectangle, a triangle, and various polygons—that have the same area (16 cm^2) as the 4 cm x 4 cm square piece. Does the shape make a difference in the force required to pull the plastic piece from the water? How can you explain your results?

Try squares made from a window screen or berry baskets that have a gridlike structure. Is the force required to pull water apart using these squares more, less, or the same as that with plastic pieces of the same area?

Design an experiment that will enable you to estimate the maximum volume of water lifted by each of the plastic pieces you have used.

4-4*
Viscosity (Thickness)

You have seen that friction is a force that opposes motion. As you might expect, there are frictional forces within liquids. It is not surprising that the molecules of a liquid, which are free to move about one another, interfere with one another's motion. The same is true of gases, but the effect is more difficult to detect and measure. These forces are called viscous forces. Viscosity, the property of being viscous, is often referred to as thickness. It is a characteristic property of liquids that can be measured in various ways. One way is to measure the time for different liquids to pass through a narrow opening. Liquids that are viscous will take longer to pass through an opening than will liquids that are less viscous. Can you explain why?

Things you will need:
- Styrofoam cups
- small nail
- a partner
- stopwatch or a watch with a second hand
- sink
- pen or pencil
- notebook
- cooking oil
- rubbing alcohol
- syrup
- molasses
- soapy water

To compare the viscosities of different liquids, you can measure the time it takes the liquids to empty from a container. A Styrofoam cup makes a convenient container because you can easily make a hole in the bottom of the cup with a small nail. Place the nail *inside* the cup and gently push it through the center of the cup's bottom to the outside.

Hold your finger over the hole while you fill the cup to a readily identifiable level with tap water at room temperature. Have a partner with a stopwatch or a watch with a second hand say "Go!" Remove your finger when you hear "Go!" Let the water empty into a sink. At the moment the water stops flowing from the cup, say

"Stop!" Your partner should then note and record the time that has elapsed since he or she started timing. Repeat the experiment several times to be sure your results are reasonably consistent. Then calculate and record the average time for water to empty from the cup.

Repeat the experiment, using cooking oil at room temperature. In this case, you will want to let the oil empty into another clean cup so that it can be reused. Is cooking oil more or less viscous than water?

Repeat the experiment, using rubbing alcohol, syrup, molasses, and soapy water. (These liquids, too, should be captured in a clean cup so that they can be reused.)

After you have completed taking all your data, examine your results. List the liquids you have tested in order of increasing viscosity.

Exploring on Your Own

Design and carry out an experiment to find out whether viscosity is affected by temperature.

Design and carry out an experiment to find out whether viscosity and density are related.

4-5
Solid or Liquid?

Not all substances are easily defined as liquid or solid. To make such a substance, put 120 mL (4 oz) of cornstarch and 60 mL (2 oz) of water in a disposable pan. Use your hands to mix the water and cornstarch. You might add a few drops of food coloring to make the mass more appealing to look at.

Things you will need:

- graduated cylinder or measuring cup
- cornstarch
- water
- disposable container
- small nail
- sheet of cardboard about 30 cm (12 in) on a side
- cover for container
- food coloring

Hold some of this strange stuff in your hand. Notice how it slips through your fingers. What happens when you try to pull it apart? When you tear it?

Use a small nail to make a hole in a sheet of cardboard. Put the strange stuff on the cardboard. Does it leak through the hole?

Play with this strange material. Test it in various ways. Does it behave like a liquid, a solid, or both?

If you want to save this substance and show it to others, store it in a covered container. If it dries, just add a little water.

5

Conductivity and the Effects of Temperature on Matter

For electrical energy to reach your home, it must travel there from a power plant. Once there, it must be able to be carried (conducted) to all the electrical appliances in your home.

Similarly, to keep your home warm, heat must be conducted from a source to the air in all the rooms of your house or apartment. Since matter provides the "highways" needed to conduct electricity and heat, it is useful to know which kinds of matter are the best conductors.

In this chapter, you will find out which kinds of matter are good conductors and which are not. You will also discover another way that heat can be transported and how temperature affects the volume of matter.

5-1*
Electrical Conductivity

Things you will need:

- flashlight batteries (D-cells)
- battery holder(s) or tape and paper clips
- insulated wires with alligator clips (if possible) or clothespins or screws
- solid objects—nails, silverware, coins, scissors, plastic, glass, wood, cardboard, candles, chalk, rubber bands, etc.
- 6-volt lantern battery
- small plastic or paper cup or vial
- different liquids—water, rubbing alcohol, vinegar, milk, fruit juices, cooking oil, solutions of salt, sugar, baking soda, Epsom salts, and alum
- seltzer tablet

As you know from experience, an electric lightbulb will not work unless there is a wire leading to and from it that connects to a source of electricity. These wires allow electric charges to flow through the bulb and heat the filament to a temperature high enough to make it glow. The flow of charge constitutes an electric current. The current travels through a conductor. Consequently, metal wires are conductors, but not all solids are conductors. Some solids do not allow charges to move through them. Such solids are called nonconductors or insulators.

To find out whether a solid is a conductor, you can use the apparatus shown in Figure 28a. One or two flashlight batteries (D-cells) can be placed in a battery holder as shown, or you can improvise your own battery holder by taping a paper clip to each pole (end) of a battery.

If you have wires with alligator clips, as shown in Figure 28a, you can clip one end of an insulated wire to each pole of the battery. If you do not have wires with alligator clips, you can use clothespins to clamp the bare ends of the wires to the ends of the battery holder or paper clips. These wires are called lead wires. Clip or screw the other end of one wire to one side of the bulb holder (socket), as shown in the drawing. The wire from the opposite end

101

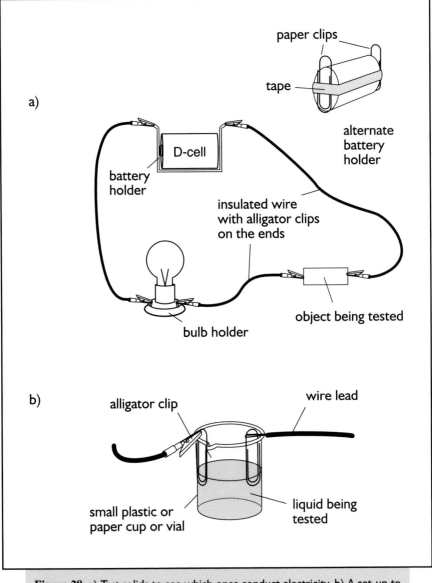

a)

paper clips

tape

alternate battery holder

D-cell

battery holder

insulated wire with alligator clips on the ends

object being tested

bulb holder

b)

alligator clip

wire lead

small plastic or paper cup or vial

liquid being tested

Figure 28. a) Test solids to see which ones conduct electricity. b) A set-up to test liquids for conductivity is shown.

of the battery can be held firmly against one end of the solid whose conductivity you are testing. A third insulated wire can be used to connect the bulb to the other end of the solid being tested.

You may have to experiment a bit to find the proper number of flashlight batteries and a bulb that lights but does not burn out. Your best bet is to touch the ends of the solid you are testing momentarily with lead wires. If the bulb glows brightly, remove the wires and reduce the number of flashlight batteries. If the bulb glows dimly, you can add batteries or find a more sensitive bulb.

Firmly, but momentarily, touch both ends of the solid you are testing with the ends of the two wires. If the bulb lights, what does it tell you about the object's ability to conduct charge? What do you know if the bulb does not light?

Test a variety of solid objects. You might try various metal objects—nails, silverware, coins, scissors, and so on, as well as solids made of plastic, glass, wood, cardboard, and various other materials such as candles and chalk.

Which of the solids you tested are conductors? Which appear to be nonconductors?

What liquids do you think will conduct electric charge? To find out, you will need to use a 6-volt lantern battery in place of the D-cell, because liquids tend to be poorer conductors than solids. Place the liquid you want to test in a small plastic or paper cup or vial. Slide two paper clips over the sides of the container, as shown in Figure 28b. The lower half of each clip should be covered with liquid. Connect one lead wire to one paper clip. Touch the other lead wire to the second paper clip.

Test a number of different liquids, such as water, rubbing alcohol, vinegar, milk, fruit juices, and cooking oil, as well as solutions of salt, sugar, baking soda, Epsom salts, and alum. If the bulb lights, what does this tell you about the liquid you are testing?

If the bulb does not light, the liquid may be a nonconductor, or it may be a poor conductor. Do you see gas bubbles forming around either of the paper clips? The bubbles show that even though there is not enough electric current to light the bulb, there is enough to cause some kind of chemical reaction around the paper clips.

How about gases? Do they conduct electricity? Using the apparatus you used to test liquids for conductivity, does current flow when the cup or vial is filled with air?

If air is not a conductor, perhaps carbon dioxide is. You can test the conductivity of carbon dioxide quite easily. Put a small volume of water in the bottom of the cup or vial. The water should not touch the paper clips. Connect the paper clips to the battery and bulb, then add a small piece of a seltzer tablet to the water. What will happen when the seltzer tablet enters the water? What gas is generated? Is carbon dioxide gas a conductor of electricity?

Exploring on Your Own

Which parts of a flashlight bulb are conductors? Is the metal side of the bulb a conductor? How about the small metal knob at the bottom of the bulb? Will the ceramic material around the metal knob conduct electricity? Which parts of a bulb must be connected to a source of electric current if the bulb is to light?

Carry out an investigation to find out why water to which salt has been added will conduct electricity but water to which sugar has been added will not.

If gases are not conductors, how does lightning move between clouds or between cloud and ground? Do some research to find out how lightning, which is a huge electric current, can move through air.

5-2
Thermal (Heat) Conductivity of Solids

The ability of a substance to conduct heat is called *thermal conductivity*. The greater the thermal conductivity of a substance, the faster heat flows through it.

Will substances that conduct electricity also conduct heat? To help you answer this question, place a metal pan and a wooden or plastic cutting board in a freezer. Which of these two objects would you expect to be a good conductor of electricity? If you are not sure, how can you find out?

After about twenty minutes, remove the metal and wooden or plastic objects from the freezer. Hold one in each hand. How can you tell which material is the better conductor of heat? Which one conducts heat more readily from your hand?

Let a hot water tap run until the water reaches its maximum temperature. Then fill a wooden

Things you will need:

- metal pan
- wooden or plastic cutting board
- freezer
- clock or watch
- hot water tap
- wooden bowl
- small metal cooking pan
- glass cooking pan
- large bucket or basin of ice water
- ice
- hot and cold tap water
- 250-mL (8-oz) steel can
- thermometer
- watch or stopwatch
- 250-mL (8-oz) glass jar or beaker about as thick as the steel can
- 7-oz Styrofoam cup
- graph paper
- pen or pencil
- notebook
- tin can, paper cup, plastic cup, and Styrofoam cups (one with a cover)

bowl, such as a salad bowl, with hot tap water. Immediately thereafter, fill a small metal cooking pan and a glass cooking pan with the hot tap water. From your results in Experiment 5-1, which of the three objects is the best conductor of electricity?

Empty the wooden bowl and turn it over. Place your hand on the dry bottom of the bowl and note how warm it feels. Repeat the procedure for the metal and glass cooking pans. Which of the three solids best conducts heat to your hand?

Substances that conduct heat poorly are called *thermal insulators.* Substances that conduct heat well are called *thermal conductors.* Which of the substances you tested—wood, glass, and metal— would you classify a conductor? Which would you classify as an insulator?

To investigate conductivity in a more quantitative way, fill a large bucket or basin to a depth of about 5 cm (2 in) with a mixture of ice and cold tap water. Then fill a 250-mL (8-oz) steel can with hot tap water and measure its initial temperature. Put the can of hot water into the ice water and use the thermometer to measure its temperature every minute until it reaches 10 °C (50 °F). Record the temperatures and times in a table.

Repeat the experiment, using a glass jar with the same amount of hot water at the same initial temperature. Perform the experiment a third time, using a Styrofoam cup.

Plot a graph of temperature versus time for each container. You can plot all three sets of data on the same graph. Examine the three curves on the graph. Which solid is the best conductor of heat? Which is the worst conductor or the best insulator? Would you want to drink hot cocoa from a steel cup? Why or why not?

Put 100 mL of hot tap water into each of five different containers—a tin can, a paper cup, a plastic cup, an insulated cup, and an insulated cup with an insulating cover. Place all five cups side by side and measure the temperature in each cup at two-minute intervals. Plot temperature versus time for each cup. Plot all the curves on the same graph.

In which cup did the water cool fastest? Slowest? Which material is the best insulator? Does a cover affect the rate at which a liquid cools?

5-3*
Thermal Conductivity of Liquids and Gases

Liquids are poor conductors of heat. To see that this is true, let a piece of ice slide to the bottom of a test tube. Slowly slide a metal washer or nut down the tube to hold the ice in place. Then add cold water to the test tube. Hold the test tube with a clamp. **Under adult supervision**, heat the water at the upper end of the test tube with a candle, alcohol burner, or Bunsen burner, as shown in Figure 29. You will find that you can make water near the top of the tube boil before the ice melts.

As you might suspect, gases are not good conductors of heat, either. To demonstrate

Things you will need:

- ice
- test tube
- metal washer or nut
- clamp to hold test tube
- an adult
- candle, alcohol burner, or Bunsen burner
- aluminum soda can
- small aluminum pan with flat bottom
- aluminum foil
- graduated cylinder or metric measuring cup
- gloves
- heavy frying pan
- stove
- an adult

the poor conductivity of air, you can use an aluminum soda can and a small aluminum muffin baking cup. If you look at the bottom of the aluminum soda can, you will see that it is not flat. Inside the bottom rim it has a domelike surface that provides an air pocket above whatever the can is resting on. The aluminum cup you use should have a flat surface. You can buy such a cup, similar to the one shown in Figure 30, in a supermarket. The cup and the can should have very nearly the same mass. If one is lighter than the other, put some aluminum foil in the lighter one to make their masses the same.

Pour 100 mL of cold water into the can and into the cup. The temperature of the water in the two containers should be the same.

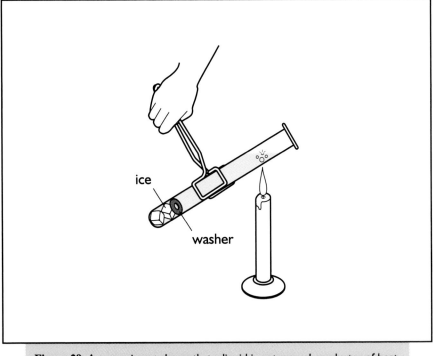

Figure 29. An experiment shows that a liquid is not a good conductor of heat.

Wearing gloves, place both the can and the cup in a heavy frying pan. **Under adult supervision**, place the frying pan on a stove's heating element and turn on the heat. Use the thermometer to stir the water in the aluminum cup occasionally. When the temperature of the water in the cup reaches approximately 40 °C (105 °F), remove both containers from the frying pan, stir the water in both containers, and record the final temperatures. Into which container was more heat conducted? How do you know? How can you account for the difference in conductivity?

Exploring on Your Own

Make some flat pieces of ice by freezing water in wide shallow plastic dishes or trays. These are some objects that you might place on

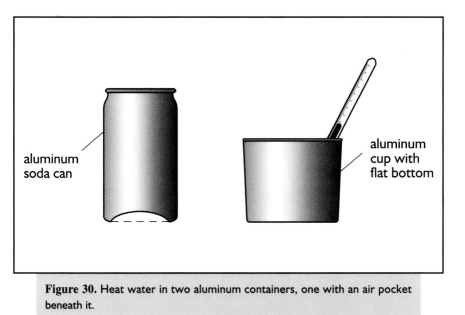

Figure 30. Heat water in two aluminum containers, one with an air pocket beneath it.

the surface of the ice: a stack of coins, a marble, a small block of wood, an eraser, a stack of metal washers, a stack of rubber washers, a plastic block, a piece of chalk. Which of those objects, if placed on the ice, do you think will conduct heat to the ice and then sink into the ice?

5-4
The Effect of Temperature on Gases and Liquids

Gases

To see what happens to a gas when it is heated, turn a large, narrow-necked, rigid plastic or glass bottle upside down. Place the mouth of the bottle under the surface of some water in a drinking glass. Warm the rest of the bottle with your hands or with a cloth soaked in hot water. What do you see emerging from the submerged mouth of the bottle? How can you explain what you observe? What happens if you cool the bottle by placing a cloth soaked in cold water on the bottle?

To further examine the effect of temperature on a gas, pull the neck of an empty balloon over the mouth of a large (1 L or larger) glass or rigid plastic bottle. Put the bottle in a pan of hot water and watch what happens. What evidence do you have that a gas expands when heated?

What do you think will happen if you put the bottle and balloon in a refrigerator for an hour or two? Try it! Were you right?

Things you will need:

- large, narrow-necked, rigid plastic or glass bottle (1 L or larger)
- cold water
- drinking glass
- cloth
- hot water
- balloon
- large glass or rigid plastic bottle (1 L or larger)
- pan of hot water
- refrigerator
- freezer
- test tube
- food coloring
- one-hole rubber stopper
- 15-cm-long piece of glass or plastic tubing
- scissors
- thin cardboard
- tape
- pencil or pen
- large plastic container
- hot tap water
- ice water
- rubbing alcohol

What do you think will happen if you transfer the bottle and balloon to a freezer for an hour? Do the results confirm your prediction?

What you saw happen to air when it was heated or cooled is true of all gases. If you were to repeat the experiment with carbon dioxide, helium, hydrogen, or any other gas, the results would be the same. Careful experiments show that any gas at 0 °C expands or contracts or expands by $\frac{1}{273}$ of its volume for each degree change in temperature. Consequently, the expansion or contraction of a gas with temperature cannot be used to identify the gas.

Liquids

To find out how liquids change when their temperatures rise or fall, fill a test tube to the brim with water to which you have added food coloring. Push a one-hole rubber stopper that holds a 15-cm-long piece of glass or plastic tubing into the mouth of the test tube. The water level should rise about halfway up the narrow tube, as shown in Figure 31.

Using scissors, cut a strip of thin cardboard to fit behind the glass tube. Tape the cardboard strip to the tube. After ten minutes, mark the water level on the cardboard, using a pencil or pen.

Put the test tube in a container filled with hot tap water. What happens to the water level in the tube?

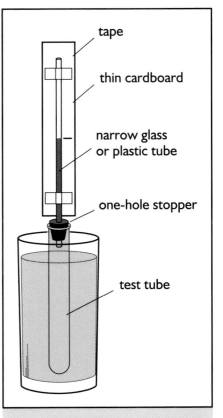

Figure 31. What happens to the volume of a liquid when its temperature rises or falls?

tape

thin cardboard

narrow glass or plastic tube

one-hole stopper

test tube

Mark the final level of the water on the cardboard. Then put the test tube into another container filled with ice water. What happens to the level of the water in the tube? Mark the final water level.

What happens to the volume of the water when the temperature increases? What happens to the volume of the water when the temperature decreases?

Repeat the above experiment with rubbing alcohol in place of water. Does alcohol expand and contract in the same way as water when its temperature changes? Are there any differences in the behavior of these two liquids when they are heated or cooled?

5-5*
The Effect of Temperature on Solids

If you have ever let hot running water flow over the screw-on lid of a jar to make it easier to open, you may know how temperature affects solids. Why would the jar be easier to open after it was heated?

You can also do an experiment to see out how solids are affected by temperature. **Ask an adult to help you, because you will be using matches and candles during the experiment.**

To begin, hammer a 10-penny nail into a point near the center of each of two wooden blocks. Then place two tables about 3 m (10 ft) apart. The blocks can be fastened to the tables with C-clamps, as shown in Figure 32.

Thread one end of a 3-m (10-ft) length of steel wire through a steel washer and wind the wire around itself several times to fasten it to the washer. Then thread a rubber band through the washer and loop its two ends over the nail in the first block. Twist the other end of the wire around the nail in the second block. Then pull the tables apart until the wire is almost straight and the rubber band is well stretched.

Bend the end of the wire near the washer so that it points straight down toward the block. Use a pencil to make a mark on the block directly under the end of the wire. Then ask two friends,

Things you will need:

- an adult
- hammer
- 10-penny nails
- ruler
- 2 wooden blocks, 5 cm x 10 cm x 30 cm (2 in x 4 in x 12 in)
- 2 tables
- C-clamps
- 3-m (10-ft) length of 18-gauge steel wire
- steel washer
- heavy rubber band
- 2 friends
- pencil
- matches
- 4 candles
- 3-m (10-ft) length of 18-gauge aluminum wire (copper or brass wire may be used in place of the aluminum or steel wire)

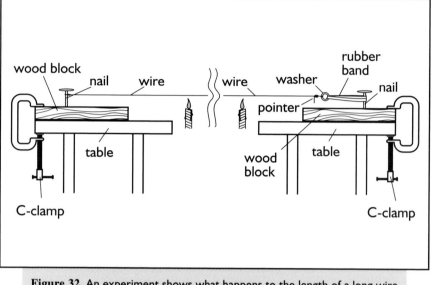

Figure 32. An experiment shows what happens to the length of a long wire when it is heated.

under adult supervision, to slowly move the flames of four lighted candles back and forth along the length of the wire while you watch the wire pointer. Does the length of the long wire change when it gets hotter? How do you know? Mark the new position of the pointer. How much did the length of the wire change?

Repeat the experiment, **under adult supervision,** using aluminum wire. Does the length of the aluminum wire change when it is heated? If it does, how does its change in length compare with that of the steel wire?

Exploring on Your Own

Find out the meaning of "linear coefficient of thermal expansion." Based on the change in length of the wires and their original lengths, determine your experimental value for the linear coefficient of thermal expansion for the metals you tested, assuming the wires reached a temperature of 150 °C.

How could you revise your experiment to obtain a more accurate value for the linear coefficient of expansion of the metals you tested?

To find the "volume coefficient of expansion" for a gas, measure the circumference of an air-filled balloon at room temperature. Record both the temperature of the room and the circumference of the balloon in degrees Celsius. Place the balloon and a thermometer in a refrigerator for about an hour. Then record the temperature in the refrigerator and the circumference of the balloon. How can you use the balloon's circumference to find its radius? Assuming the balloon to be spherical, how can you find the volume of the gas in the balloon? How much did the volume of the balloon change per degree change in temperature? By what fraction of its original volume did the volume of air change for each degree change in the Celsius temperature?

Investigate some practical applications of the expansion of substances when heated. You might begin with thermometers and thermostats, but there are many more.

What are some practical precautions that must be taken due to the fact that materials used in construction expand or contract with changes in temperature?

Galileo is believed to have built the world's first thermometer. Find out how he used the expansion and contraction of a gas to measure temperature. Then build a thermometer similar to his. What problems are associated with such a thermometer?

5-6*
Water's Strange Behavior

As you have seen, solids, liquids, and gases contract when cooled and expand when heated. In general, if you cool a liquid to the point where it freezes, it contracts during the freezing process and will continue to contract if the solid is cooled further. As a result, the density of the substance increases as its temperature falls, and the solid state is more dense than the liquid state. But water behaves very differently than most substances.

Things you will need:

- transparent plastic drinking straw
- drinking glass
- water
- food coloring
- clay
- small jar
- marking pen
- freezer
- clock or watch

To see that this is true, place a transparent plastic drinking straw in a glass of water that has been colored with a drop or two of food coloring. Place your finger firmly on the top of the straw, as shown in Figure 33. If you keep your finger on top of the straw, the water will stay in the straw when you lift it out of the glass.

While keeping your finger on the top of the straw, press the bottom of the straw into a lump of clay at the bottom of a small jar. If you remove your finger from the straw now, the water should remain in place.

Once you are sure water is not leaking from the straw, mark the water level in the straw with a marking pen. Put the jar that holds the water-filled straw into a freezer. After about 30 minutes, open the freezer and look at the water level in the straw. Has the water turned to ice? What happened to the volume as the liquid water changed to solid ice? How do you know that the solid ice is less dense than the liquid water from which it came?

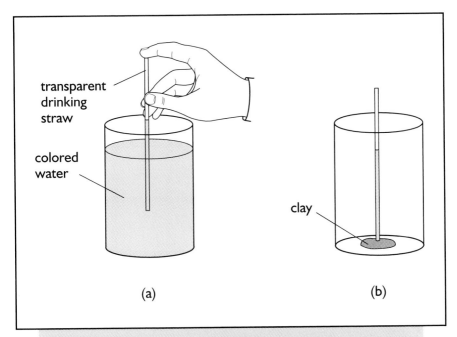

transparent drinking straw

colored water

clay

(a)

(b)

Figure 33. a) A drinking straw can be used as a pipette to remove water from a container. b) The water can be kept in the straw by using clay to seal off the bottom of the straw. The water can then be transferred to a freezer.

Exploring on Your Own

Investigate the significance of water's abnormal behavior as it changes from a liquid to a solid. What would happen to lake and pond life if water behaved like other substances when it froze?

Investigate the meaning of "turnover" as it applies to what takes place in many lakes and ponds during autumn and spring. How is the abnormal behavior of water related to the turnover of lakes and ponds?

Design an experiment to find the temperature at which water reaches its maximum density of 1.0 g/cm³. What happens to the density of ice as it cools to temperatures below its freezing point?

5-7*
Convection

You have found that liquids and gases are not good conductors of heat. But why are water and air used in heating systems? One possible explanation might be that the density of substances such as air and water are related to temperature. Perhaps density differences can be used to transport heat.

To check this idea, nearly fill a clear plastic vial with cold water. Add a drop of food coloring to another vial and fill it with hot water. Now use an eyedropper to remove some of the hot colored water. Next, place

Things you will need:
- clear plastic vials
- cold water
- food coloring
- hot water
- eyedropper
- thermometer
- heated room
- pen or pencil
- notebook
- hammer
- small nail
- small jar
- large, clear, tall glass or plastic container

the tip of the eyedropper very close to the bottom of the vial of cold water. Very gently squeeze the hot water out into the bottom of the cold water, as shown in Figure 34. What happens? What does this tell you about the density of hot water compared with that of cold water?

Repeat the experiment, but this time nearly fill a clear plastic vial with hot water. Add a drop of food coloring to another vial and fill it with cold water. Very gently squeeze the colored water out into the bottom of the hot water. What happens? What does this tell you about the density of cold water compared with hot water? What do you think will happen if you release the cold water near the top of the hot water? Try it! Were you right?

Perhaps temperature affects the density of air and other gases in the same way it affects liquids. To find out, measure the temperature

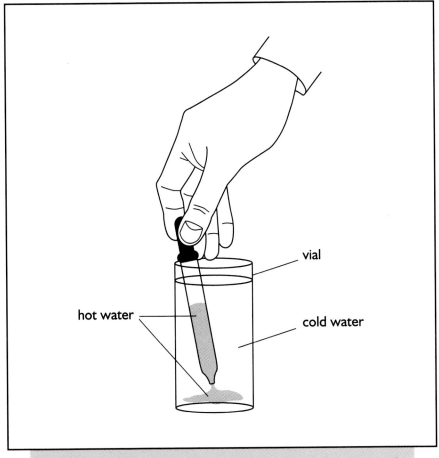

vial

hot water

cold water

Figure 34. Very gently release some hot colored water onto the bottom of a vial nearly full of clear, cold water.

near the floor of a room. Be sure the liquid level in the thermometer is not changing before you record the temperature. Then put the thermometer near the ceiling above an inside wall of the same room. After the temperature stops changing, record it. How do the two temperatures compare? What does this tell you?

The movement of fluids resulting from differences in density due to temperature is called convection. Convection currents can be found in the ocean, and in the atmosphere, where they give rise to winds. The wind that you may feel at the beach on a summer afternoon is caused by warm air over the land rising and being replaced by cooler, denser air coming off the water.

To see convection currents on a small scale, use a hammer and a small nail to punch two holes in the lid of a small jar. A jar such as one in which samples of jelly are sold works well. Next, fill a large, clear, tall glass or plastic container with very cold water. Add a few drops of food coloring to the small jar and then fill it to the

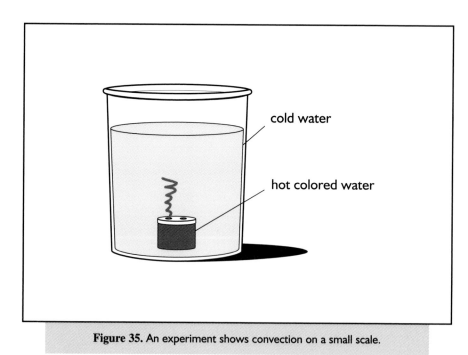

cold water

hot colored water

Figure 35. An experiment shows convection on a small scale.

brim with very hot water. Screw the lid with the two holes onto the small jar and place it on the bottom of the large container of cold water, as shown in Figure 35.

Watch closely. You will see the colored hot water emerge from the top of the small jar. What happens to this water after it leaves the jar? Try to explain what you observe. Why does the convection you are observing stop after a few minutes?

Exploring on Your Own

Investigate the role of convection in the hot-water and hot-air heating systems used to keep buildings warm in the winter.

What is the significance of 4 °C as it relates to the convection of water in lakes and ponds?

List of Suppliers

Carolina Biological Supply Co.
2700 York Road
Burlington, NC 27215
(800) 334-5551; <http://www.carolina.com>

Central Scientific Co. (CENCO)
3300 Cenco Parkway
Franklin Park, IL 60131
(800) 262-3626; <http://www.cenconet.com>

**Connecticut Valley Biological
Supply Co., Inc.**
82 Valley Road, P.O. Box 326
Southampton, MA 01073
(800) 628-7748

Delta Education
P.O. Box 915
Hudson, NH 03051-0915
(800) 258-1302

Edmund Scientific Co.
101 East Gloucester Pike
Barrington, NJ 08007
(609) 547-3488

Educational Innovations, Inc.
151 River Road
Cos Cob, CT 06807-2514
<http://www.teachersource.com>

Fisher Science Education
485 S. Frontage Road
Burr Ridge, IL 60521
(800) 955-4663; <http://www.fisheredu.com>

Frey Scientific
100 Paragon Parkway
Mansfield, OH 44903
(800) 225-3739

Nasco-Fort Atkinson
P.O. Box 901
Fort Atkinson, WI 53538-0901
(800) 558-9595

Nasco-Modesto
P.O. Box 3837
Modesto, CA 95352-3837
(800) 558-9595; <http://www.nascofa.com>

Sargent-Welch/VWR Scientific
P.O. Box 5229
Buffalo Grove, IL 60089-5229
(800) SAR-GENT; <http://www.SargentWelch.com>

Science Kit & Boreal Laboratories
777 East Park Drive
Tonawanda, NY 14150-6782
(800) 828-7777; <http://sciencekit.com>

Ward's Natural Science Establishment, Inc.
P.O. Box 92912
Rochester, NY 14692-9012
(800) 962-2660; <http://www.wardsci.com>

Further Reading

Adams, Richard, and Robert Gardner. *Ideas for Science Projects.* Revised edition. Danbury, Conn.: Franklin Watts, Inc., 1997.

————. *More Ideas for Science Projects.* Revised edition. Danbury, Conn.: Franklin Watts, Inc., 1998.

Bochinski, Julianne Blair. *The Complete Handbook of Science Fair Projects.* New York: John Wiley & Sons, 1996.

Bombaugh, Ruth. *Science Fair Success, Revised and Expanded.* Springfield, N.J.: Enslow Publishers, Inc., 1999.

Gardner, Robert. *Science Projects About Methods of Measuring.* Springfield, N.J.: Enslow Publishers, Inc., 1999.

————. *Science Projects About Chemistry.* Hillside, N. J.: Enslow Publishers, Inc., 1994.

Krieger, Melanie Jacobs. *How to Excel in Science Competitions: Revised and Updated.* Springfield, N.J.: Enslow Publishers, Inc., 1999.

Loeschnig, Louis V. *Simple Chemistry Experiments with Everyday Materials.* New York: Sterling Publishing Company, 1995.

Markle, Sandra. *The Young Scientist's Guide to Successful Science Projects.* New York: Lothrop, Lee and Shepard, 1990.

Mebane, R., and T. R. Rybolt. *Adventures with Atoms and Molecules: Chemistry Experiments for Young People. Books I–V.* Springfield, N.J.: Enslow Publishers, Inc., 1998.

Newton, David E. *Making and Using Scientific Equipment.* New York: Franklin Watts, Inc., 1993.

Smith, Norman F. *How to Do Successful Science Projects.* Revised edition. New York: Julian Messner, 1982.

Tocci, Salvatore. *How to Do a Science Fair Project.* Revised edition. Danbury, Conn.: Franklin Watts, Inc., 1997.

Van Cleave, Janice Pratt. *Chemistry for Every Kid: 101 Easy Experiments that Really Work.* New York: John Wiley & Sons, 1989.

Internet Addresses

Bentor, Yinon. *Chemical Elements.com.* 1996–1998. <http://www.chemicalelements.com> (January 12, 2000).

CHEMystery: An Interactive Guide to Chemistry. 1996 <http://library.advanced.org/3659> (January 12, 2000).

The Exploratorium. *Exploratorium Home Page.* 1999. <http://www.exploratorium.edu> (January 12, 2000).

The Franklin Institute Science Museum. 1995–1999. <http://sln.fi.edu/> (January 12, 2000).

Morano, David. *Guide to Doing Science Fair Projects.* May 27, 1995. <http://www.isd77.k12.mn.us/resources/cf/SciProjIntro. html> (January 12, 2000).

Rader, Andrew. *Chem4Kids.* 1997–2000. <http://www.chem4kids. com/> (January 12, 2000).

Index